Hans-Otto Blaeser

Taschenwörterbuch
——— der ———
Personalarbeit

Die wichtigsten Fachbegriffe in

deutsch — englisch

englisch — deutsch

von **A** bis **Z**

DATAKONTEXT-VERLAG

CIP-Titelaufnahme der Deutschen Bibliothek

Blaeser, Hans-Otto:
Taschenwörterbuch der Personalarbeit : d. wichtigsten
Fachbegriffe in dt.-engl., engl.-dt. von A - Z / Hans Otto
Blaeser. — Erstausg. — Köln : Datakontext-Verl., 1989
    ISBN 3-921899-89-3

NE: HST

Erstausgabe
ISBN 3-921899-89-3
Alle Rechte vorbehalten
© 1989 by DATAKONTEXT-VERLAG GmbH
Aachener Straße 1052, D-5000 Köln 40
Ohne ausdrückliche Genehmigung des Verlages ist es nicht gestattet,
das Buch oder Teile daraus in irgendeiner Form zu vervielfältigen.
Lizenzausgaben sind nach Vereinbarung möglich.
Druck: Grafischer Betrieb Karl Plitt, Oberhausen
Printed in Germany

Vorwort

Im Zuge der zunehmenden internationalen wirtschaftlichen Verflechtungen und der wachsenden Zusammenarbeit der Unternehmen über die Ländergrenzen hinweg, hat sich ein ständiger Austausch von Informationen auf dem Gebiet des Personalwesens entwickelt. Dieser Austausch, der im Rahmen der Vollendung des europäischen Binnenmarktes an Bedeutung gewinnen wird, vollzieht sich auf verschiedene Weise.

Da sind einmal die zahlreichen Publikationen, die Themen der Personalarbeit zum Inhalt haben, zum anderen aber auch der Gedanken- und Erfahrungsaustausch bei internationalen Veranstaltungen und Kongressen sowie der direkte Kontakt mit Vertretern des Personalwesens anderer Unternehmen im Ausland.

Das vorliegende Taschenwörterbuch ist für die Betriebspraktiker im Personalwesen bestimmt, die in der englischen Sprache kommunizieren müssen. Es soll ihnen helfen, bei den am häufigsten vorkommenden Wörtern und Begriffen die richtige Übersetzung zu finden. Es umfaßt Begriffe des Personalwesens im weitesten Sinne. Auch die gebräuchlichsten Begriffe der Rechtssprache, insbesondere des Arbeitsrechts, sind enthalten. Wortneuschöpfungen sind ohne Angabe ihrer Stammwörter oft schwierig zu verstehen. Deshalb wurden Stammwörter dort angegeben, wo es notwendig oder hilfreich erschien.

Dieses Wörterbuch setzt, seiner Bestimmung entsprechend, Grundkenntnisse in beiden Sprachen voraus. Bei seiner Verwendung ist zu berücksichtigen, daß die Aufgaben des Personalwesens und damit auch die Fachsprache sich ändern. Neue Techniken kommen zur Anwendung, neue Tätigkeiten entstehen, und neue Vorschriften werden erlassen, für die neue Fachausdrücke und Redewendungen gebildet werden. Aus diesem Grunde kann ein solches Wörterbuch nie vollständig sein.

Herausgeber und Verlag sind daher für Anregungen zur Ergänzung und Verbesserung sowie für Hinweise auf Irrtümer dankbar. Der Verlag nimmt solche Vorschläge gerne entgegen, damit sie bei späteren Auflagen gegebenenfalls berücksichtigt werden können.

Köln, September 1988   Herausgeber und Verlag

Hinweise für den Benutzer

— Stichwörter sind grundsätzlich alphabetisch geordnet, fettgedruckt und durch Absatz voneinander getrennt.

— Über die Einordnung eines Wortes oder seine Unterordnung unter ein Stichwort entschied der Grad seiner Selbständigkeit.

— Das Stichwort ist von seinen Übersetzungen durch einen waagerechten Strich getrennt. Die Übersetzung für die Untergruppen eines Stichwortes folgt nach einem Doppelpunkt.

— Gibt es für ein Stichwort mehrere Übersetzungen, so sind diese durch ein Komma getrennt.

— Ein Schrägstrich trennt Synonyme eines Wortes oder Ausdrucks. Die unmittelbar vor oder hinter dem Schrägstrich stehenden Synonyme können ausgetauscht werden, ohne daß sich die Bedeutung des Wortes oder Ausdrucks ändert.

— Pluralformen sind hinsichtlich ihrer alphabetischen Anordnung wie Singularformen behandelt. Sie sind durch *(Pl)* gekennzeichnet.

— Im Deutsch-Englischen Teil wurde den englischen Verben ein „to" vorangestellt, im Englisch-Deutschen Teil wurden sie durch *(v)* gekennzeichnet. Auf die Kennzeichnung der deutschen Verben wurde in beiden Teilen verzichtet.

— Männliche Substantive im Deutschen, die eine handelnde oder ausführende Person bezeichnet, enden vielfach in der weiblichen Form auf „-in". In diesem Fall ist die Endung „-in" in runde Klammern gesetzt.

z. B. Arbeiter(in) *(m ⟨f⟩)*

— Wenn im Deutschen die Endung eines männlichen Substantives vom Gebrauch des bestimmten oder unbestimmten Artikels abhängt, ist das Wort mit der Endung aufgeführt, die nach dem Gebrauch des unbestimmten Artikels folgt.

z. B. Handlungsreisender *(m)*

Diese Form steht dann sowohl für „der Handlungsreisende" als auch „ein Handlungsreisender".

- Endet im Deutschen ein Substantiv sowohl in der weiblichen als auch in der männlichen Form gleich, so ist es aufgeführt als

  z. B. Angestellte(r) *(f ⟨m⟩)*
  wobei diese Form steht für **der, die** und **eine** Angestellte, sowie **ein** Angestellter.

- Runde Klammern

  ○ nach einem Stichwort umschließen die Bezeichnung des Numerus *(Pl)*, *(Sg)* und der Wortart *(adj)*, *(adv)*, *(v)*

  ○ umschließen ganze Wörter oder Silben, die mitgelesen oder ausgelassen werden können ohne daß sich der Sinn des Wortes oder des Begriffs verändert. z. B. Förder(ungs)unterricht

  ○ umschließen innerhalb eines Wortes einzelne Buchstaben oder Silben, die eine weitere Schreibweise des Wortes darstellen. z. B. labo(u)r.

- Eckige Klammern umschließen eine Erläuterung oder Erweiterung eines Wortes oder Begriffs.

Erläuterungen der angewandten Abkürzungen
Explanation of abbreviations used

adj.	— Adjektiv	— adjective
adv.	— Adverb.	— adverb
AE	— hauptsächlich in den Vereinigten Staaten gebräuchlich	— chiefly used in the U. S.
Ausdr.	— Ausdruck	— expression
BE	— hauptsächlich in Großbritannien gebräuchlich	— chiefly used in the U. K.
bes.	— besonders	— especially
colloq.	— Umgangssprache	— colloquial
etc.	— et cetera	— and so on
f	— Feminium/weiblich	— feminine
jmd.	— jemand(en)	— someone
jur.	— juristisch	— legal
m	— Masculinum/männlich	— masculine
med.	— medizinisch	— medical
mil.	— militärisch	— military
n	— Neutrum/sächlich	— neuter
o., one's	— ein, eines	— one, one's
o. s.	— sich (selbst)	— oneself
Pl.	— Plural/Mehrzahl	— plural
Sg.	— Singular/Einzahl	— singular
s. o.	— jemand	— someone
s. th.	— etwas	— something
techn.	— technisch	— technical
v	— Verb	— verb

A

Abendkursus *(m)* — evening classes *(Pl)*, night school.

abfinden — to satisfy, to pay (off), to pay s. o. compensation, to indemnify; durch Vergleich abfinden: to compound with.

Abfindung *(f)* — compensation, indemnification, indemnity; ⟨*eines Arbeitnehmers:*⟩ dismissal compensation, redundancy/separation payment, severance pay/benefit; ⟨*eines Gläubigers:*⟩ satisfaction; ⟨*durch Vergleich:*⟩ composition.

Abfindungsplan *(m)* — redundancy scheme.

Abgaben *(f, Pl)* ⟨*soziale*⟩ — social security contributions.

Abgangszeugnis *(n)* — ⟨*eines(r) Angestellten:*⟩ clearance card, ⟨*einer Schule:*⟩ leaving certificate, diploma ⟨*AE*⟩.

Abgeltungsbetrag *(m)* — imdemnity, redemption money.

Abitur *(n)* — examination for the General Certificate of Education ⟨*BE*⟩, high-school graduation ⟨*AE*⟩.

Abkommen *(n)* — agreement: gütliches Abkommen: amicable settlement; Abkommen mit den Gewerkschaften: union contract/agreement; ein Abkommen treffen: to come to an agreement, to reach an understanding, to make a deal.

Abmahnung *(f)* — rebuke, reprimand.

Abrechnung *(f)* — (statement of) account.

Abschied *(m)* — leave; seinen Abschied nehmen: to resign, to retire, to tender one's resignation, to send in one's paper.

Abschlagszahlung *(f)* — payment on account.

Abschluß *(m)* — ⟨*einer Angelegenheit:*⟩ conclusion, ⟨*einer Debatte:*⟩ closure, completion ⟨*Fertigstellung*⟩, settlement ⟨*Vereinbarung*⟩.

Abschlußvollmacht *(f)* — contractual power, authority to negotiate/to contract.

Abschreibung *(f)* — depreciation ⟨*Wertminderung*⟩; Abschreibung an Maschinen: depreciation on machinery.

Abstimmung *(f)* — voting, vote; geheime Abstimmung: (secret) ballot.

Abteilung *(f)* — ⟨*eines Betriebes:*⟩ department, ⟨*einer Verwaltung:*⟩ section, division.

Abteilungsleiter *(m)* — department manager, department(al) head, section chief.

Abteilungsversammlung *(f)* — department meeting.

abwerben — to entice/to poach employees; to lure/to pirate labo(u)r into other jobs.

Abwerbung *(f)* — ⟨*von Angestellten:*⟩ enticement, ⟨*von Arbeitskräften:*⟩ labo(u)r piracy, ⟨*innerhalb eines Betriebes:*⟩ poaching of staff.

Abwesenheit *(f)* — absenteeism, absence (from work).

Abwesenheitsrate *(f)* — absenteeism rate.

Achtstundentag ⟨*m*⟩ — eight-hour day, 8 hr day.

Akademiker *(m)* — university man.

Akademikerausbildung *(f)* — graduate education.

akademisch *(adj)* — academical; akademischen Grad besitzen: to hold a degree; akademischen Grad verleihen: to graduate; akademische Vorbildung: academical qualification.

Akkord *(m)* — piecework, job work, tut *〈BE〉*; im Akkord arbeiten: to work by the piece/job, to do job work/piecework; im Akkord bezahlt werden: to be paid by the job; jmd. im Akkord beschäftigen: to put s. o. on piecework.

Akkordarbeiter *(m)* — piece (rate) worker, job worker, task worker, jobbing hand.

Akkordbezahlung *(f)* — piecework pay, contract wage payment.

Akkordlohn *(m)* — piece rate pay.

Akkordprämie *(f)* — piece rate bonus.

Akkordsatz *(m)* — piece rate formula, contract wage payment.

Akkordsystem *(m)* — piece rate plan, piecework system.

Akkordverdienst *(m)* — piecework rate/ earnings.

Akkordzettel *(m)* — job ticket.

Akkordzuschlag *(m)* — piecework bonus, make-up pay.

Aktionär *(m)* — shareholder.

Aktionärsvertreter *(m) 〈im Aufsichtsrat〉* — shareholder representative.

Alkoholverbot *(n)* — order to obstain from alcohol (med), prohibition (jur).

Allgemeinbildung *(f)* — general knowledge; gute Allgemeinbildung: general/ liberal education.

Allgemeinverbindlichkeit *(f) 〈eines Tarifvertrages〉* — general obligation *〈of a tariff agreement〉*.

Altersaufbau *(m)* — age distribution/ structure.

Altersfreibetrag *(m)* — age allowance/ exemption/relief.

Altersfürsorge *(f)* — retirement provisions.

Altersgrenze *(f)* — age limit; flexible Altersgrenze: flexage, flexible age limit.

Altersrente *(f)* — old-age/retirement pension.

Altersversicherung *(f)* — old-age pension fund *〈Kasse〉*.

Altersversorgung *(f) 〈betriebliche〉* — *〈company's〉* pension scheme.

Alters- und Hinterbliebenenversorgung *(f)* — old-age and survivors' insurance.

Amt *(n)* — office; ein Amt antreten: to accede/to come into/to enter upon/to take office; ein Amt aufgeben: to relinquish/to resign/to vacate office; ein Amt innehaben: to hold/to keep/to bear an office.

Amtsgericht *(n)* — ordinary district court.

Amtspflichtverletzung *(f)* — prevarication.

Änderungskündigung *(f)* — notification of a change (of the terms of employment), notice of termination for change of employment conditions.

Anfangseinkommen *(n)* — original income.

Anfangsgehalt *(n)* — initial/starting salary, starting/entrance rate.

Anfangslohn *(m)* — entrance/starting rate.

Anfechtung *(f)* — contesting; *〈eines Vertrages:〉* avoidance, recission/repudiation of a contract.

Anfechtungsgrund *(m)* — invalidating cause, cause for recission.

Anforderung *(f)*; − demand, request; den Anforderungen *(Pl)* nicht genügen: not to come up to standard; hohe Anforderungen *(Pl)* an jmd. stellen: to require a great deal of s. o.

Angebot *(n)* − offer.

angelernt − semi-skilled.

angestellt *(adj)* − employed; 〈im Büro:〉 black coated 〈BE〉, white collar 〈AE〉; bei jmd. angestellt sein: to be in s.one's pay.

Angestellte(r) *(f⟨m⟩)* − salaried employee 〈BE〉/employee 〈AE〉, white collar worker 〈colloq〉; die Angestellten *(Pl)* eines Betriebes: the staff, the salaried personnel; die leitenden Angestellten *(Pl):* senior staff, management; leitender Angestellter: manager, managerial employee; ganztägig beschäftigte(r) Angestellte(r): fulltime employee; hochbezahlte(r) Angestellte(r): high salaried employee; hochqualifizierte(r) Angestellte(r): top calibre employee; Angestellte(r) in leitender Stellung: executive (officer); außertariflicher Angestellte(r): exempt employee.

Angestelltengewerkschaft *(f)* − white-collar union.

Angestelltenverhältnis *(n)* − (salaried) employment, employee status, salaried employment status; im Angestelltenverhältnis stehen: to be employed/in salaried employment.

Angestelltenversicherungsgesetz *(n)* − Salaried Employees' Insurance Act.

Angestelltenvertretung *(f)* − salaried employee representation.

Anhörungsrecht *(n)* − 〈des Betriebsrates〉 − right to be heard.

anleiten − to instruct.

Anlernberuf *(m)* − semi-skilled occupation.

anlernen − to give initial instruction to,

to instruct, to train, to teach.

Anlernling *(m)* − trainee, learner.

Anlernlohn *(m)* − learner's wage rate.

Anmeldung *(f)* 〈zu einem Kursus〉 − enrol(l)ment, enlistment.

Annahmeverzug *(m)* − default in accepting.

anordnen − to order, to direct.

Anrechnungsklausel *(f)* − off-setting provision.

Anspruch *(m)* − claim, interest, right 〈Anrecht〉, demand, call 〈Forderung〉, entitlement; begründeter Anspruch: sound claim; verjährter Anspruch: state demand, outlawed claim; Anspruch auf Schadensersatz: claim for damages; Anspruch anerkennen: to admit/to allow/ to recognize a claim; Anspruch bestreiten: to defend/to resist/to contest a claim.

anspruchsberechtigt *(adj)* sein − to become eligible, to have a claim, to be entitled.

Anstellung *(f)* − employment, job, position, engagement, recruitment 〈AE〉, enlistment 〈Einstellung〉, appointment 〈Ernennung〉.

Anteil *(m)* − share, portion; Anteil am Gewinn: profit share; Anteil am Gesellschaftsvermögen: share/capital interest in a partnership.

Anteilseigner *(m)* − shareholder 〈BE〉, stockholder 〈AE〉.

Anwartschaft *(f)* − expectancy, candidacy, qualification 〈Befähigung〉, 〈für Versicherung:〉 qualifying period, prospective entitlement.

anweisen − to direct, to order 〈anordnen〉, to assign, to allot 〈zuweisen〉.

anwerben − to enlist, to recruit 〈AE〉, to hire.

Anwerbung *(f)* 〈von Arbeitskräften〉 −

engagement, enlistment, enrol(l)ment, recruitment ⟨AE⟩.

Anwesenheitsprämie *(f)* — attendance premium/bonus.

Anzeige *(f)* — advertisement.

Anzeigepflicht *(f)* — obligation to report.

anzeigepflichtig *(adj)* — notifiable, reportable.

Arbeit *(f)* — employment, achievement, job, occupation ⟨*Beschäftigung*⟩, work, labo(u)r, task, assignment ⟨*Aufgabe*⟩, workmanship, craftsmanship, handwork ⟨*Ausführung*⟩, service ⟨*Dienst*⟩, performance, output ⟨*Leistung*⟩, effort, trouble, pains ⟨*Mühe*⟩; anstrengende Arbeit: trying work; geistige Arbeit: brainwork; körperliche Arbeit: physical/ manual work; leichte Arbeit: light work; schwere Arbeit: hard work/labo(u)r; schwierige Arbeit: tough job; ungelernte Arbeit: unskilled work; schlechte Arbeit leisten: to tinker; sich an die Arbeit machen: to settle down to work, to set to work, to get to business; Arbeit suchen: to look for a job, to seek work/ employment; Tag der Arbeit: May Day/ Labor Day ⟨AE⟩, Arbeit haben: to be employed, to have a job; keine Arbeit haben: to be unemployed/out of work; Arbeit wiederaufnehmen: to resume work; Arbeit niederlegen/einstellen: to lay down tools/to stop working, to knock off; jmd. von der Arbeit abhalten: to keep s. o. from his work; Arbeit auf Prämienbasis: work on the bonus system; Arbeit unter Tariflohn: scab work.

arbeiten — to (be at) work, to serve ⟨*dienen*⟩, to produce, to make, to manufacture ⟨*herstellen*⟩; im Akkord arbeiten: to work by the job, to do job-work; am Fließband arbeiten: to work on the assembly line; ganztägig arbeiten: to work full time; umschichtig arbeiten: to take turns.

Arbeiter *(m)* — worker, workman, labo(u)rer ⟨*bes. ungelernter Arbeiter*⟩, ⟨*an einer Maschine:*⟩ operator, die Arbeiter *(Pl)* ⟨*Arbeitskräfte*⟩: labo(u)r force, manpower; angelernter Arbeiter: semi-skilled worker; gewerblicher Arbeiter: manual worker; im Stundenlohn beschäftigter Arbeiter: hourly (paid) worker; qualifizierter Arbeiter: qualified worker; überzähliger Arbeiter: redundant worker; unbeschäftigte Arbeiter *(Pl)*: idle workmen; ungelernter Arbeiter: unskilled worker, plug ⟨*colloq*⟩.

Arbeiterbewegung *(f)* — labo(u)r movement.

Arbeiterfamilie *(f)* — working-class family.

Arbeiterklasse *(f)* — working class.

Arbeitgeber *(m)* — employer; Verhältnis zwischen Arbeitgeber und Arbeitnehmer: industrial relations ⟨AE⟩, labo(u)r-management relations.

Arbeitgeberanteil *(m)* ⟨*zur Sozialversicherung*⟩ — employers' contribution.

Arbeitgeberverband *(m)* — employers' association.

Arbeitnehmer *(m)* — employee, organisierte Arbeitnehmer *(Pl)*: unionized employees.

Arbeitnehmer - Arbeitgeber - Beziehungen *(f, Pl)* — labo(u)r-management relations, industrial relations ⟨AE⟩.

Arbeitnehmeranteil *(m)* ⟨*zur Sozialversicherung*⟩ — employees' contribution.

Arbeitnehmererfindung *(f)* — employee invention.

Arbeitnehmerfreibetrag *(m)* — earned-income allowance.

Arbeitnehmerpflichten *(f, Pl)* — employee obligations *(Pl)*.

Arbeitnehmer-Sparzulage *(f)* — employee saving allowance.

Arbeitnehmerüberlassung *(f)* — manpower provision.

Arbeitnehmerüberlassungsgesetz *(n)* — Manpower Provision Act ⟨= *Act respecting the provision of manpower as a commercial operation*⟩.

Arbeitnehmervertreter *(m)* — employee representative.

Arbeitnehmervertretung *(f)* — employee representation.

Arbeitsablauf *(m)* — work flow/routine, working process, sequence of operations ⟨*techn*⟩.

Arbeitsablaufplan *(m)* — flow chart.

Arbeitsamt *(n)* — (un)employment office, labor office ⟨*AE*⟩, labour exchange ⟨*BE*⟩; Internationales Arbeitsamt: International Labo(u)r Office (ILO); sich beim Arbeitsamt melden: to report at the (un)employment office.

Arbeitsanalyse *(f)* — job/position analysis.

Arbeitsanzug *(m)* — working clothes *(Pl)*.

Arbeitsauftrag *(m)* — work/job order.

Arbeitsausfall *(m)* — loss of working hours/time.

Arbeitsbedingungen *(f, Pl)* — ⟨*arbeitsvertragliche:*⟩ employment conditions, ⟨*äußere:*⟩ working conditions.

Arbeitsbefreiung *(f)* — release/exemption from working, time off.

Arbeitsbeginn *(m)* — commencement of work, starting time; verschiedene Zeiten für den Arbeitsbeginn festlegen: to stagger starting times.

Arbeitsbelastung *(f)* — workload.

Arbeitsbericht *(m)* — work/job report, performance report.

Arbeitsbereich *(m)* — work area.

Arbeitsbereitschaft *(f)* — stand-by-time.

Arbeitsbeschaffungsmaßnahme *(f)* — make-work scheme, job creating measure.

Arbeitsbeschaffungsprogramm *(n)* — employment scheme, relief program(me).

Arbeitsbescheinigung *(f)* — employment certificate, ⟨*nach Entlassung:*⟩ discharge paper.

Arbeitsbewertung *(f)* — job/position evaluation.

Arbeitsdirektor *(m)* — labo(u)r/workers' director.

Arbeitseifer *(m)* — eagerness for/to work, work urge.

Arbeitseinkommen *(n)* — earned income, personal earnings.

Arbeitseinsatz *(m)* — employment of labo(u)r, placement, labo(u)r allocation: ⟨*Arbeitszuweisung*⟩.

Arbeitsentgelt *(n)* — pay, renumeration.

Arbeitsessen *(n)* — working lunch, working dinner, business luncheon, meeting session.

Arbeitserlaubnis *(f)* — work permit.

Arbeitsersparnis *(f)* — labo(u)r saving.

arbeitsfähig *(adj)* — able to work, fit for work.

Arbeitsfähigkeit *(f)* — employability, ability to perform, capacity to work.

Arbeitsfolge *(f)* — sequence of operations, work sequence.

Arbeitsförderungsgesetz *(n)* — Employment Promotion Act.

arbeitsfrei *(adj)* — free of work, (work)free; arbeitsfreier Tag: day off; einen arbeitsfreien Tag nehmen: to take a day off.

Arbeitsfrieden *(m)* — industrial peace.

Arbeitsgang *(m)* — process, working process ⟨*Verfahren*⟩.

Arbeitsgebiet *(n)* — field/sphere of business/work.

Arbeitsgenehmigung *(f)* — work permit.

Arbeitsgerät *(n)* — implement(s).

Arbeitsgericht *(n)* — labo(u)r court, industrial tribunal ⟨*BE*⟩.

Arbeitsgerichtsbarkeit *(f)* — labo(u)r jurisdiction, jurisdiction over industrial matters.

Arbeitsgerichtsgesetz *(n)* — Labo(u)r Court Act.

Arbeitsgesetzgebung *(f)* — labo(u)r legislation.

Arbeitsgruppe *(f)* — team, working party ⟨*BE*⟩.

Arbeitshöchstzeit *(f)* — maximum working hours.

Arbeitshygiene *(f)* — industrial hygiene.

Arbeitsinhalt *(m)* — job/work content.

arbeitsintensiv *(adj)* — labo(u)r intensive.

Arbeitskampf *(m)* — industrial action, labo(u)r dispute.

Arbeitskleidung *(f)* — work dress, work(ing) clothes.

Arbeitskollege *(m)* — associate ⟨*Berufs-/Standeskollege*⟩, colleague, fellow worker, workmate.

Arbeitskonflikt *(m)* — labo(u)r/industrial conflict.

Arbeitskosten *(Pl)* — labo(u)r/employment cost.

Arbeitskraft *(f)* — worker, workman: ⟨*Arbeiter*⟩, working capacity; menschliche Arbeitskraft: manpower; weibliche Arbeitskraft: female/woman worker.

Arbeitskräfte *(f, Pl)* — manpower; Arbeitskräfte abbauen: to reduce the labo(u)r force; Arbeitskräfte einsparen: to save labo(u)r; Arbeitskräfte umsetzen: to dislocate labo(u)r.

Arbeitskräfteabbau *(m)* — cutback on manpower.

Arbeitskräftebedarf *(m)* — demand for employees/workers, manpower requirement.

Arbeitskräftemangel *(m)* — labo(u)r shortage.

Arbeitskräfteüberschuß *(m)* — redundant labo(u)r.

Arbeitsleistung *(f)* — efficiency ⟨*Leistungskraft, Leistungsergebnis*⟩, man-hours ⟨*aufgewandte Zeit*⟩, performance ⟨*Arbeitsleistung einer Person*⟩, productivity; working capacity ⟨*Leistungsfähigkeit*⟩.

Arbeitslohn *(m)* — pay, wage, wages.

arbeitslos — idle, jobless, workless, not occupied, unemployed, out of employ/job/work; arbeitslos werden: to fall/to be thrown out of work, to be made redundant, to be dismissed, to be sacked.

Arbeitslosenfürsorge *(f)* — unemployment relief.

Arbeitslosengeld *(n)* — unemployment benefit.

Arbeitslosenhilfe *(f)* — unemployment relief.

Arbeitslosenquote *(f)* — level of unemployment, unemployment rate.

Arbeitslosenrate *(f)* — unemployment rate.

Arbeitslosenunterstützung *(f)* — unemployment benefit/compensation/pay/relief; Arbeitslosenunterstützung beziehen: to draw unemployment benefit, to be/to live on the dole ⟨*colloq*⟩, to receive unemployment compensation.

Arbeitsloser *(m)* — unemployed person.

Arbeitslosigkeit *(f)* — unemployment; Rückgang der Arbeitslosigkeit: drop in unemployment; konjunkturelle Arbeitslosigkeit: cyclical unemployment; langfristige Arbeitslosigkeit: long-run/long-term unemployment; saisonbedingte Arbeitslosigkeit: seasonal unemployment; strukturelle Arbeitslosigkeit: structural unemployment; temporäre Arbeitslosigkeit: frictional unemployment.

Arbeitsmangel *(m)* − shortage/lack of work.

Arbeitsmarkt *(m)* − labo(u)r market.

Arbeitsmedizin *(f)* − industrial medicine.

Arbeitsmethode *(f)* − method of work/operation, operational method, working system.

Arbeitsministerium *(n)*− Ministry of Labour *⟨BE⟩*, Department of Labor *⟨AE⟩*, Labor Department *⟨AE⟩*.

Arbeitsmoral *(f)* − (working) morale, employee morale.

Arbeitsniederlegung *(f)* − downing tools, strike, walkout *⟨AE⟩*, work stoppage.

Arbeitsordnung *(f)* − shop/work regulations.

Arbeitsorganisation *(f)* − work(ing) organisation.

Arbeitsort *(m)*− place of work, duty station.

Arbeitspapiere *(n, Pl)* − employment/working papers.

Arbeitspause *(f)* − break, rest period, pause, recess *⟨AE⟩*.

Arbeitsplan *(m)* − (working) schedule/scheme.

Arbeitsphysiologie *(f)* − occupational physiology.

Arbeitsplatz *(m)* − place of work, yard *⟨AE⟩*, work(ing) place, job *⟨Stelle⟩*; seinen Arbeitsplatz wechseln: to change one's job; seinen Arbeitsplatz häufig wechseln: to job-hop; nicht an seinem Arbeitsplatz sein: to be off work; freier Arbeitsplatz: vacancy; sicherer Arbeitsplatz: safe place to work; unbesetzter Arbeitsplatz: job vacancy.

Arbeitsplatzbeschreibung *(f)* − job/position description, job specification *⟨AE⟩*.

Arbeitsplatzbewertung *(f)* − job/position evaluation.

Arbeitsplatzgestaltung *(f)* − workplace/job layout, job engineering *⟨inhaltliche Gestaltung⟩*, human engineering *⟨AE⟩*, job design, ergonomics.

Arbeitsplatzschutz *(m)* − job security/protection.

Arbeitsplatzsicherheit *(f)*−job security.

Arbeitsplatzwechsel *(m)*− *⟨im Betrieb:⟩* transfer, *⟨zu einem anderen Betrieb:⟩* turnover; geplanter abwechselnder Arbeitsplatzwechsel: job rotation.

Arbeitsprozeß *(m)* − working process; jmd. wieder in den Arbeitsprozeß eingliedern: to put s. o. back to work, to rehabilitate s. o.

Arbeitspsychologie *(f)*− industrial psychology.

Arbeitsrecht *(n)*− labor law *⟨AE⟩*, industrial law *⟨BE⟩*.

Arbeitsrichter *(m)* − labo(u)r court judge.

arbeitsscheu *(adj)* − adverse to labo(u)r, dodging *⟨BE⟩*, workshy.

Arbeitsschicht *(f)*− (work) shift.

Arbeitsschluß *(m)* − end/close of work, knocking-off time *⟨colloq⟩*.

Arbeitsschutz *(m)*− industrial safety.

Arbeitsschutz(be)kleidung *(f)* − protective clothing.

Arbeitsschutzgesetz *(n)* − protective labor law *⟨AE⟩*, workers' protection law.

Arbeitssicherheit *(f)* − occupational safety.

Arbeitssicherheitsgesetz *(n)* ⟨= *Gesetz über Betriebsärzte, Sicherheitsingenieure und andere Fachkräfte für Arbeitssicherheit*⟩ — Act respecting plant physicians, safety engineers and other occupational safety specialists.

Arbeitssicherheits-Fachkraft *(f)* — (occupational) safety specialist.

Arbeitsstätten-Richtlinien *(f, Pl)* — workplaces rules.

Arbeitsstätten-Verordnung *(f)* — Workplace Regulations/Ordinance.

Arbeitsstellenmarkt *(m)* — job market.

Arbeitsstoff *(m)* — substance to be used in connection with work.

Arbeitsstunde *(f)* — manhour: ⟨*als Produktionseinheit*⟩, working hour.

Arbeitssuchender *(m)* — employment/ job applicant, job seeker.

Arbeitstag *(m)* — office day, working day, workday ⟨*AE*⟩.

Arbeitstakt *(m)* — ⟨*am Fließband:*⟩ production cycle, ⟨*an einer Maschine:*⟩ working cycle.

Arbeitsteilung *(f)* — division of labo(u)r/ employment.

Arbeitstempo *(n)* — work speed.

Arbeitsüberlastung *(f)* — overwork.

Arbeitsumgebung *(f)* — layout of workplaces.

arbeitsunfähig *(adj)* — disabled, incapable of work, unable/unfit to work, unemployable; dauernd arbeitsunfähig: invalid, permanently unemployable; vorübergehend arbeitsunfähig: incapable of work(ing), temporarily incapacitated; arbeitsunfähig geschrieben werden: to be returned unfit for work.

Arbeitsunfähigkeit *(f)* — inability to work, disablement, unfitness for work, unemployability, incapacity to/for work/from

working; dauernde Arbeitsunfähigkeit: permanent disability; vorübergehende Arbeitsunfähigkeit: temporary disablement.

Arbeitsunfähigkeitsbescheinigung *(f)* — certificate of disability.

Arbeitsunfall *(m)* — accident at work, industrial/work accident, occupational injury.

Arbeitsunterbrechung *(f)* — work stoppage.

Arbeitsverhältnis *(n)* — employment relationship; befristetes Arbeitsverhältnis: temporary employment; faktisches Arbeitsverhältnis: de facto/actual employment relationship; im Arbeitsverhältnis stehen: to be (gainfully) employed (with); sein Arbeitsverhältnis lösen: to terminate one's employment.

Arbeitsvermittlung *(f)* — finding of employment, procurement of work.

Arbeitsversäumnis *(n)* — absence from work, ⟨*langandauernd:*⟩ absenteeism.

Arbeitsvertrag *(m)* — employment/labo(u)r contract.

Arbeitsverweigerung *(f)* — refusal to work.

Arbeitsverzögerung *(f)* — delay, slowdown.

Arbeitsvorbereitung *(f)* — industrial engineering, operations scheduling.

arbeitswillig *(adj)* — willing to work.

Arbeitswissenschaft *(f)* — ergonomics, ergonomic science.

Arbeitszeit *(f)* — working time/hours, company time; flexible Arbeitszeit: flextime, flexible working hours; gestaffelte Arbeitszeit: staggering of hours; nachgeholte Arbeitszeit: make-up work; normale Arbeitszeit: straight time; verkürzte Arbeitszeit: part time employment, short/part time; Arbeitszeit registrieren: to clock; während der Arbeitszeit: on company time; außerhalb der Arbeitszeit: on employee time.

Arbeitszeitordnung *(f)* — Working Time Regulation.

Arbeitszeitverkürzung *(f)* — reduction of working hours, working time reduction.

Arbeits(-zeit)vorgaben *(f, Pl)* — work standards.

Arbeitszeug *(n)* — equipment, tools.

Arbeitszeugnis *(n)* — testimonial, reference, certificate.

Arbeitszufriedenheit *(f)* — job/work satisfaction.

Arbeitszuweisung *(f)* — labo(u)r allocation.

ärztlich *(adj)* — medical; ärztliche Untersuchung: medical examination; ärztliche Versorgung: medical care; ärztliches Zeugnis: doctor's/medical certificate.

Aufenthaltserlaubnis *(f)* — ⟨für Ausländer:⟩ alien's residence permit, registration certificate; residence permit.

Aufgabe *(f)* — duty, function, business, job, office, task; responsibility ⟨Pflicht⟩; eine Aufgabe erfüllen: to perform a task; eine Aufgabe erledigen: to tackle a job; einer Aufgabe gewachsen sein: to be up to one's job; berufliche Aufgabe: job assignment; ehrenamtliche Aufgaben *(Pl)*: honorary duties.

Aufgabenanreicherung *(f)* — job enrichment.

Aufgabenbereich *(m)* — scope of duties, function, sphere of action, field of activity; einen neuen Aufgabenbereich übernehmen: to enter upon new duties; jmd. einen Aufgabenbereich zuweisen: to assign a duty to s. o.

Aufgabenerweiterung *(f)* — job enlargement.

Aufgabenzuweisung *(f)* — job assignment.

Aufgliederung *(f)* — breakdown ⟨AE⟩, splitting up; berufliche Aufgliederung: occupational distribution; Aufgliederung nach Sachgebieten: functional classification.

Aufhebungsvertrag *(m)* — cancel(l)ation contract.

Aufkündigung *(f)* ⟨der Dienste⟩ — notice to quit.

Aufrechnung *(f)* — set off ⟨BE⟩, offset ⟨AE⟩.

Aufsicht *(f)* — control, inspection, superintendence, supervision, guardianship ⟨vormundschaftliche Aufsicht⟩, surveillance ⟨Polizeiaufsicht⟩, ärztliche Aufsicht: medical care; Aufsicht führen/die Aufsicht haben: to superintendend, to supervise.

Aufsichtsbehörde *(f)* — supervisory authority.

Aufsichtsperson *(f)* — supervisor, person in charge.

Aufsichtsrat *(m)* — supervisory board (of a German-type public limited company), board of supervision.

Aufsichtsratsvergütung *(f)* — directors' fees.

aufsteigen ⟨Karriere⟩ — to advance.

Aufstiegsmöglichkeit *(f)* — career opportunity, opportunity for promotion; Stellung ohne Aufstiegsmöglichkeit: dead-end job.

Aufteilung *(f)* — breakdown ⟨AE⟩.

Aufwandsentschädigung *(f)* — expense allowance.

Aufwendungen *(f, Pl)* — expenditure, expense.

Ausbildung *(f)* — ⟨im weiteren Sinne:⟩ education, ⟨in/auf einem Gebiet:⟩ instruction, ⟨Schulung zu etwas:⟩ training; Ausbildung am Arbeitsplatz: on the job training ⟨AE⟩; akademische Ausbildung: academic training, university education.

Ausbildungsabschluß *(m)* — completion of one's education.

Ausbildungsbeihilfe *(f)* — training/education grant, training subsidy.

Ausbildungsnachweis *(m)* — educational certificate.

Ausbildungsvertrag *(m)* — training contract.

Ausfallzeit *(f)* — ⟨*Versicherung:*⟩ inactive period, ⟨*Arbeitszeit:*⟩ down time, hours lost.

Ausgleichsabgabe *(f)* ⟨*nach dem Schwerbehinderten-Gesetz*⟩ — equalization pay for non employment of disabled persons, equalization contribution.

aushandeln — to bargain for, to negotiate, to settle; endgültig aushandeln: to come to terms on.

Aushang *(m)* — ⟨*formell:*⟩ bulletin; notice.

Aushangbrett *(n)* — bulletin/notice board.

Aushilfe *(f)* — temporary help/assistance.

Aushilfsarbeitsverhältnis *(n)* — temporary employment relationship.

Aushilfskraft *(f)* — stopgap, temporary worker/help, auxiliary (worker).

Auslagen *(f, Pl)* — outlay, expenses; Auslagen ersetzen/zurückerstatten: to

refund s.one's expenses, to reimburse s. o. (for) his expenses.

Auslagenerstattung *(f)* — expense reimbursement.

Auslandsaufenthalt *(m)* — stay abroad.

Auslandserfahrung *(f)* — experience acquired abroad.

auslernen — to complete one's training/ ⟨*Lehrling:*⟩ apprenticeship, to finish learning.

Ausleseprüfung *(f)* — competitive examination.

Ausleseverfahren *(n)* — process of selection, screening system.

Ausschlußfrist *(f)* — term/time of preclusion.

Ausschreibung *(f)* (von Stellen) — advertisement (of a vacancy).

Ausschuß *(m)* *(für)* — committee *(on)*.

Außendienstzulage *(f)* — field allowance.

Aussperrung *(f)* — lockout.

Auswahl *(f)* — selection; soziale Auswahl: social selection.

auswählen — to select.

Auswahlrichtlinie *(f)* — selection guideline.

Auswahltest *(m)* — selection test.

Auszeichnung *(f)* — award.

Auszubildende(r) (AZUBI) *(f⟨m⟩)* — apprentice.

B

Bandarbeit *(f)* — moving-line production, (belt) line production.

Bandbesetzung *(f)* — manning of moving lines, line manning.

Bandgeschwindigkeit *(f)* — (moving) line speed.

Bargeld *(n)* — cash, ready money.

bargeldlos *(adj)* — cashless.

Barzahlung (f) — cash payment, payment in cash.

Baudarlehen (n) — building loan.

Bearbeitungssystem (n) — processing system.

Beendigung (f) ⟨des Arbeitsverhältnisses durch Kündigung⟩ — termination.

Befähigung (f) (zu) — ability, capability, fitness, qualification (for).

Beförderung (f) ⟨eines Arbeitnehmers⟩ — promotion.

befördern zu — to promote (to be), to promote to the position of.

befristen — to deadline s. o., to limit s. o. as to time, to place a time limit on s. o.; befristetes Arbeitsverhältnis: temporary employment.

Befristung (f) — deadline, time limit.

begabt (adj) — gifted, talented.

Begabtenförderung (f) — financial assistance to the gifted.

Begabung (f) — gift, talents (Pl), aptitude.

behindert (adj) — disabled, handicapped; geistig behindert: mentally handicapped/retarded; körperlich behindert: physically handicapped.

Beisitzer (m) — assessor, associate judge, lay judge: ⟨Laienrichter⟩.

Beitragspflicht (f) — compulsory contribution, liability to contribute.

Belegschaft (f) — personnel, employees, workers, workforce, staff ⟨BE⟩.

Belohnung (f) — award.

Bemessungsgrundlage (f) — basis for assessment.

Benachteiligung (f) — discrimination.

Berechnungsgrundlage (f) — basis for calculation.

Bereitschaftsdienst (m) — stand-by duty, emergency service.

Beruf (m) — job ⟨Tätigkeit⟩; occupation ⟨Beschäftigung⟩, profession ⟨höherer Beruf⟩, trade ⟨kaufm./handwerk./allg.⟩, vocation ⟨Berufung⟩; einen Beruf ausüben: to carry/to follow a trade, to exercise a profession, to persue an occupation; einen Beruf ergreifen: to go into trade, to take up a profession; den Beruf verfehlt haben: to have missed one's vocation; Arzt von Beruf: a physician by profession; von Beruf Mechaniker: a mechanic by trade.

beruflich (adj) — occupational, professional, vocational; beruflich verhindert: detained by work; beruflich verreist: away on business; beruflich (hier) zu tun haben: to be (here) on business.

Berufsaussichten (f, Pl) — professional/job prospects.

Berufsauffassung (f) — professional ethics (Pl.).

Berufsausbildung (f) — professional education, vocational training.

Berufsberatung (f) — job counseling, vocational counseling/guidance.

Berufsberatungsstelle (f) — vocational advice department/guidance center.

Berufsbezeichnung (f) — job nomenclature, job title ⟨AE⟩, occupational name.

Berufsbildung (f) — occupational education.

Berufsbildungsgesetz (n) — Vocational Education Act, Vocational Training Act.

Berufserfahrung (f) — work/professional experience.

Berufsförderung (f) — vocational advancement.

berufsfremd (adj) — non occupational, unrelated to one's vocation/profession.

Berufsgenossenschaft *(f)* — employers' liability insurance association: professional/trade association, workmen's compensation office.

Berufsgruppe *(f)* — occupational group.

Berufskleidung *(f)* — working clothes.

Berufskollege *(m)* — associate.

Berufskrankheit *(f)* — occupational disease/illness, industrial disease.

Berufsrisiko *(n)* — occupational hazard/risk.

Berufsschule *(f)* — (part-time) vocational school, industrial/technical/trade school.

berufsunfähig *(adj)* — disabled, unfit to work.

Berufsunfähigkeit *(f)* — disability.

Berufsunfall *(f)* — occupational accident/injury.

Berufsverbot *(n)* — professional ban.

Berufsvertretung *(f)* — professional representation.

Berufswahl *(f)* — occupational decision, vocational choice.

Berufung *(f)* ⟨*jur*⟩ — appeal ⟨*on facts and law*⟩ (gegen: against, from; bei: to).

beschäftigen — to employ, to occupy.

beschäftigt sein — to be in employment/in the employ by of, to be on the pay roll, to be employed by; ganzzeitig beschäftigt sein: to be employed on a fulltime basis.

Beschäftigtenstand *(m)* — level of employment.

Beschäftigte(r) *(f⟨m⟩)* — employee, employed person.

Beschäftigung *(f)* — employment ⟨*Anstellung*⟩, job; bisherige Beschäftigung: former/previous employment/occupation; geregelte Beschäftigung haben: to have regular work/a regular job.

Beschäftigung *(f)* — activity ⟨*Tätigkeit*⟩, occupation, work, pursuit, business.

Beschäftigungsart *(f)* — employment category.

Beschäftigungsbedingungen *(f, Pl)* — employment conditions.

Beschäftigungsförderungsgesetz *(n)* — Employment Promotion Act.

Beschäftigungslage *(f)* — *(level of)* employment, labo(u)r (-market) situation.

beschäftigungslos *(adj)* — unemployed, out of work, out of a job ⟨*colloq*⟩.

Beschäftigungslosigkeit *(f)* — unemployment.

Beschäftigungsnachweis *(m)* — certificate of employment.

Beschäftigungspflicht *(f)* — employment obligation.

Beschäftigungsstand *(m)* — level of employment.

Beschäftigungsverhältnis *(n)* — employment relationship.

Bescheinigung *(f)* — attestation, certificate, certification; ärztliche Bescheinigung: medical certificate.

Beschwerde *(f)* — complaint, reclamation; förmliche Beschwerde ⟨*jur*⟩: petition for review.

Beschwerdefall *(m)* — employee grievance, (subject of) complaint.

Beschwerdeführer *(m)* — complainer, claimant.

Beschwerdestelle *(f)* — grievance committee.

Beschwerdeverfahren *(n)* — appeal procedure ⟨*Verfahrensweise*⟩, appeal proceedings ⟨*Verhandlung*⟩, ⟨*für Arbeitnehmer:*⟩ grievance procedure.

Besetzung *(f)* ⟨*personelle*⟩ — manning.

besolden — to salary, to pay.

Besoldung *(f)* — salary.

Bestätigung *(f)* — confirmation.

Bestätigungsschreiben *(n)* — letter of confirmation.

Betreuung *(f)* — care, caretaking; ärztliche Betreuung: medical care.

Betrieb *(m)* — operation, business (manufacturing) plant, factory *⟨Betriebsanlage⟩*, kontinuierlicher Betrieb: continuous operation; firm, establishment; einen Betrieb leiten: to run a plant; einen Betrieb schließen: to close a plant; einen Betrieb verlagern: to relocate.

betrieblich *(adj)* — operational, operating, operative.

betriebliche Altersversorgung *(f)* — company's pension scheme.

betriebliche Übung *(f)* — estblished operating practices.

Betriebsablauf *(m)* — operative procedure.

Betriebsabteilung *(f)* — staff/business department.

Betriebsänderung *(f)* — plant/works alteration.

Betriebsarzt *(m)* / **Betriebsärztin** *(f)* — company doctor/physician.

Betriebsausfall *(m)* — breakdown, operating trouble, stoppage.

Betriebsausflug *(m)* — works/staff outing.

Betriebsausschuß *(m)* *⟨des Betriebsrates⟩* — works committee.

betriebsbedingt *(adj)* — operational; betriebsbedingte Kündigung: dismissal for operational reasons.

Betriebsberater *(m)* — company consultant.

Betriebsbesichtigung *(f)* — plant tour/visit.

Betriebsbuchhaltung *(f)* — cost accounting.

Betriebseinschränkung *(f)* — short-time working.

Betriebserfindung *(f)* — employee's invention.

Betriebsferien *(f)* — plant shut-down.

Betriebsgefahr *(f)* — operational risk/hazard.

Betriebsgeheimnis *(n)* — trade secret; ein Betriebsgeheimnis verraten: to divulge a trade secret.

Betriebsgelände *(n)* — plant site.

Betriebsgemeinkosten *(Pl)* — indirect cost, overhead.

Betriebshaftpflichtversicherung *(f)* — manufacturer's public liability, workmen's compensation insurance *⟨Berufsgenossenschaft⟩*.

Betriebsingenieur *(m)* — industrial engineer.

Betriebsjubiläum *(n)* — company anniversary.

Betriebsklima *(n)* — atmosphere at work.

Betriebskrankenkasse *(f)* — plant health insurance, works sickness fund.

Betriebsleiter *(m)* — works/operations manager, plant manager.

Betriebsleitung *(f)* — senior staff, (plant) management.

Betriebsordnung *(f)* — works regulations.

Betriebsrat *(m)* — works/workers' council.

Betriebsratsmitglied *(n)* — works council member.

Betriebsrente *(f)* — company pension.

Betriebsrentengesetz *(n)* *⟨= Gesetz zur Verbesserung der betrieblichen Alters-*

versorgung⟩ — Act to Improve Works Old-age Pension Coverage.

Betriebsschließung *(f)* — shutdown.

Betriebsstillegung *(f)* — close down, plant closing/closure.

Betriebsteil *(m)* — seperate department.

Betriebsumfrage *(f)* — employee attitude survey.

Betriebsunfall *(m)* — industrial accident/injury, working accident; meldepflichtiger Betriebsunfall: reportable accident in industry; tödlicher Betriebsunfall: industrial fatality.

Betriebsvereinbarung *(f)* — works agreement.

Betriebsverfassung *(f)* — works constitution.

Betriebsverfassungsgesetz *(n)* — Works Constitution Act.

Betriebsverlegung *(f)* — plant relocation.

Betriebsversammlung *(f)* — employee/works meeting, works assembly.

Betriebszeitung *(f)* **/ Betriebszeitschrift** *(f)* — company magazine, personnel periodical.

Betriebszugehörigkeit *(f)* — length of (company) service, length of continuous employment, seniority employment, seniority ⟨AE⟩; Betriebszugehörigkeit anrechnen: to allow service.

beurlauben — to give/to grant s. o. leave, to give s. o. time off; sich beurlauben lassen: to take one's leave.

Beurlaubung *(f)* — granting s. o. leave, lay off ⟨*vorübergehende Entlassung wegen Arbeitsmangel*⟩.

beurteilen — to rate, to assess ⟨*Leistung*⟩, to judge.

Beurteilung *(f)* — report, rating, performance rating ⟨*Leistung*⟩, appraisal.

bevorschussen — to advance.

bewähren, (sich) — to prove o. s.

Bewährungszeit *(f)* — probationary period/term, probation.

bewegungseingeschränkt — mobility-impaired.

bewerben, (sich) *(um, für)* — to apply *(for)*, to stand; sich bei einer Firma um eine Anstellung bewerben: to apply to a firm for a position/job.

Bewerber *(m)* — *(job)* applicant, candidate.

Bewerbung *(f)* — application.

Bewerbungsformular *(n)* — application blank ⟨AE⟩/form.

Bewerbungsunterlagen *(f, Pl)* — application papers.

Bezahlung *(f)* — pay, payment, compensation ⟨*Entschädigung*⟩.

Bezüge *(m, Pl)* — earnings, emoluments, income.

Bilanz *(f)* — balance sheet.

Bildschirmgerät *(n)* — visual display unit (VDU).

Bildung *(f)* — culture, refinement, knowledge ⟨*Kenntnisse*⟩, learning, (formal) education ⟨*feine Bildung*⟩.

Bildungschancen *(f, Pl)* — educational opportunities.

bildungsfähig *(adj)* — ⟨*Mensch:*⟩ educ(at)able/capable of being educated, ⟨*Geist:*⟩ cultivable/capable of being developped.

Bildungsmangel *(m)* — illiteracy, unrefinement.

Bildungsniveau *(n)* — educational level.

Bildungsurlaub *(m)* — eductional/study leave.

Bildungsweg *(m)* — educational channel; „Zweiter Bildungsweg": the second way of gaining university admission.

Billigkeitsgrundsatz *(m)* — principle of equity.

Bordvertretung *(f)* — ship's committee.

Briefwahl *(f)* — postal ballot.

Bruttolohn *(m)* — gross wage/earnings *(Pl)*.

Bruttostundenverdienste *(m, Pl)* — gross hourly wages.

Buchhalter(-in) *(m⟨f⟩)* — bookkeeper, bookkeeping clerk.

Buchhändler *(m)* — bookseller, book-dealer *⟨AE⟩*.

Buchprüfer *(m)* — accountant, auditor.

bummeln *⟨bei der Arbeit⟩* — to slack at one's work.

Bummelstreik *(m)* — go-slow, slow down *⟨AE⟩*.

Bundesanstalt für Arbeit *(f)* — Federal Employment Institution.

Bundesarbeitsgericht *(n)* — Federal Labo(u)r Court.

Bundesarbeitsminister *(m)* — Federal Minister of Labo(u)r.

Bundesfinanzhof *(m)* — Federal Finance Court.

Bundesgesetzblatt *(n)* — Federal Gazette.

Bundeskindergeldgesetz *(n)* — Federal Family Allowance Act *⟨= Act respecting the grant of family and education supplement⟩*.

Bundesurlaubsgesetz *(n)* — Federal Leave Act *⟨= Act to provide for a minimum period of leave for workers⟩*.

Bundesverband der Deutschen Industrie *(m)* — Confederation of German Industry.

Bundesvereinigung der Deutschen Arbeitgeberverbände *(f)* — Federation of the German Employers' Associations.

Bundesverfassungsgericht *(n)* — Federal Constitutional Court.

Bundesversicherungsanstalt für Angestellte *(f)* — Federal Social Insurance Institution for (Sarlaried) Employees.

Bundeswehr *(f)* — German Federal Armed Forces.

Büro *(n)* — office.

Büroangestellte(r) *(f⟨m⟩)* — office clerk, clerical employee.

Büroeinrichtung *(f)* — office equipment.

Bürogehilfe *(m)* — clerical assistant, office boy.

Büropersonal *(n)* — clerical staff.

Bürovorsteher *(m)* — office keeper, chief/head/senior clerk.

C

Chancengleichheit *(f)* — equal opportunities *(Pl)*

Charakter *(m)* — nature, character.

Charakterbeurteilung *(f)* — estimate of a person's character.

Charakterfestigkeit *(f)* — strength of character, moral strength.

Chef *(m)* — employer, head, chief, boss; Chef sein: to boss.

D

Daten *(n, Pl)* — data, particulars ⟨*Personalangaben*⟩.

Datenverarbeitung *(f)* — data processing.

Dauerarbeitslosigkeit *(f)* — chronic/persistant unemployment.

Dauerbeschäftigung *(f)* — permanent occupation/employment, constant employment.

Dauerstellung *(f)* — permanent post/position/employment.

delegieren — to delegate.

Deutsche Angestelltengewerkschaft *(f)* — German Salaried Staff Union.

Deutscher Gewerkschaftsbund *(m)* — Confederation of the German Trade Unions.

Deputat *(n)* — allowance in kind.

Diäten *(Pl)* — emoluments ⟨*Tagegeld*⟩ per diem allowance, attendance fee ⟨*Sitzungsgeld*⟩.

Dienst *(m)* — service, work, office, duty; Dienst nach Vorschrift: work-to-rule, go-slow ⟨*BE*⟩; seinen Dienst antreten: to enter the employ; außer Dienst: out of office, retired form office; aus dem Dienst entlassen: to dismiss, to remove from office, to fire.

Dienstalter *(n)* — length/years of service, seniority ⟨*AE*⟩.

Dienstaltersprinzip *(n)* — seniority system.

Dienstanweisung *(f)* — instruction, procedure.

Dienstantritt *(m)* — assumption of office, starting of work, entry into service.

Dienstaufsicht *(f)* — supervision.

Dienstgespräch *(n)* — official/business call.

Dienstjubiläum *(n)* — employment/business anniversary.

dienstlich *(adj)* — official; dienstlich verhindert sein: to be detained by business.

Dienstpflicht *(f)* — official duty.

Dienstreise *(f)* — official/business trip, travel on official business; auf Dienstreise sein: to travel on duty.

Dienststellung *(f)* — employment status.

diensttauglich *(adj)* — able-bodied.

Dienstunfähigkeit *(f)* — disablement.

Dienstverhältnis *(n)* — employment relationship.

Dienstvertrag *(m)* — employment contract.

Dienstwagen *(m)* — company car.

Dienstwohnung *(f)* — company flat.

Dienstzeugnis *(n)* — testimonial, reference, certificate.

Diplom *(n)* — certificate, diploma.

Diplomarbeit *(f)* — thesis.

Diplom-Ingenieur *(m)* — civil/certified engineer.

Diplomkaufmann *(m)* — Bachelor of Commerce ⟨*BE*⟩.

Direktionsrecht *(n)* — right to give directions.

Direktor *(m)* — director; kaufmännischer Direktor: director of business affairs.

Direktversicherung *(f)* — direct insurance coverage.

Disziplinarbestimmungen *(f, Pl)* — disciplinary procedures.

Disziplinarfall *(m)* – disciplinary case.

Disziplinarstrafe *(f)* – disciplinary penalty/punishment.

Doktorand(in) *(m⟨f⟩)* – candidate for scholastic hono(u)rs, doctorand, doctoral candidate.

Doktorarbeit *(f)* – (doctoral) thesis/dissertation.

Doktorexamen *(n)* – promotional examination.

Doktortitel *(m)* – doctorate, doctor's degree.

Doppelarbeitsverhältnis *(n)* – double employment (relationship).

Drogenmißbrauch *(m)* – drug abuse.

Drückeberger *(m)* ⟨colloq⟩ ⟨bei der Arbeit⟩ – slacker.

durchfallen ⟨im Examen⟩ – to fail/to flunk ⟨AE⟩ in an examination, to be plucked ⟨BE⟩.

E

Ecklohn *(m)* – tariff corner rate, pilot rate.

Effektivität *(f)* – effectiveness.

Effektivlohn *(m)* – actual wage, take home pay, net wage/earnings.

Ehefrau *(f)* – wife, spouse; mitarbeitende Ehefrau: working wife.

Ehegatte *(m)* / **Ehegattin** *(f)* – marital partner; überlebende(r) Ehegatte/Ehegattin: surviving espouse.

ehelich *(adj)* – marital, matrimonial, legitimate ⟨Kind⟩; ehelich geboren: born in wedlock; eheliches Kind: legitimate child.

Ehestandsbeihilfe *(f)* – marriage grant.

Ehestandsdarlehen *(n)* – marriage loan.

Ehrenamt *(n)* – honorary post/office/function.

ehrenamtlich *(adj)* – honorary, unpaid.

Ehrengericht *(n)* – court of hono(u)r.

ehrenrührig *(adj)* – discreditable, defamatory.

Ehrgeiz *(m)* – ambition.

Eid *(m)* – oath, affidavit; an Eides Statt: in lieu of an affidavit/oath; einen Eid erklären/leisten: to execute an affidavit, to make an affirmation.

Eignung *(f)* – suitability, qualification, fitness.

Eignungsprüfung *(f)* – qualification test, qualifying examination; betriebliche Eignungsprüfung: employment test.

Eignungsuntersuchung *(f)* ⟨med⟩ – fitness test.

einarbeiten – ⟨jmd:⟩ to instruct/to train s. o. for, ⟨sich:⟩ to familiarize o. s. with/to acquaint o. s..

Einarbeitungszeit *(f)* – period of vocational adjustment.

Einbehaltung *(f)* – ⟨von Abgaben, Steuern:⟩ retention, deducation, ⟨von Gewerkschaftsbeiträgen:⟩ checkoff ⟨AE⟩, deducation of union dues.

Einberufungsbefehl *(m)* – conscription order, draft/induction order ⟨AE⟩.

eingruppieren – to classify, to group.

Eingruppierung *(f)* – classification.

einigen, sich – to get together, to agree, to settle, to come to an agreement.

Einigung *(f)* − settlement, agreement, understanding.

Einigungsstelle *(f)* − conciliation committee.

Einkommen *(n)* − income, emolument ⟨*Einkünfte*⟩, earnings ⟨*Erträge*⟩; berufliches Einkommen: professional income; steuerbares/steuerpflichtiges Einkommen: taxable income, assessable income ⟨*AE*⟩.

Einmalzahlung *(f)* − once-for-all-payment.

Einsatz *(m)* ⟨*von Personal*⟩ − placement, employment, assignment of labo(u)r.

Einschichtbetrieb *(m)* − single shift operation.

Einsparung *(f)* − saving; Einsparung von Arbeitskräften: saving of labo(u)r, headcount saving.

einstellen − to engage, to employ, to recruit ⟨*AE*⟩, to hire ⟨*AE*⟩; Arbeit einstellen: to stop working, to lay down tools.

Einstellung *(f)* ⟨*von Personal*⟩ − hiring, engagement, recruitment.

Einstellungsbedingungen *(f, Pl)* − employment conditions.

Einstellungsgespräch *(n)* − hiring interview.

Einstellungsstop *(m)* − hiring freeze.

Einstellungstermin *(m)* − starting date.

Einstufung *(f)* − classification, employee rating ⟨*AE*⟩; Einstufung nach der Leistungsfähigkeit: performance rating; Einstufung in eine höhere Lohngruppe: promotional classification; Einstufung in eine niedrigere Lohngruppe: demotional classification.

Einstufungsgruppe *(f)* − grade, rating.

einverständlich *(adj)* − by mutual consent.

einweisen − to instruct, to brief.

Einwohnermeldeamt *(n)* − population register, registration office.

Einzelakkord *(m)* − single piecework.

Einzelarbeitsplatz *(m)* − individual workplace.

Einzelarbeitsvertrag *(m)* − individual employment contract.

Einzelnachweis *(m)* − specification.

Einzelprokura *(f)* − single/sole procuration.

Einzelunterricht *(m)* − private lessons.

Einzugsgebiet *(n)* − labo(u)r market area.

Elektroinstallateur *(m)* − electrician.

Elektrotechniker *(m)* − electrical engineer.

Elementarzeiten *(f, Pl)* − standard elemental times.

Elementarzeitbestimmungssystem *(n)* − method-time measurement („MTM").

Empfehlungsbrief *(m)* − letters of commendation *(Pl)*, commendatory letter.

Entgelt *(n)* − payment, pay, remuneration ⟨*Belohnung*⟩, compensation ⟨*Wiedergutmachung*⟩.

entlassen − to dismiss, to discharge, to sack ⟨*colloq*⟩, to pay off, to fire ⟨*AE*⟩; vorübergehend entlassen: to lay off; fristlos entlassen: to dismiss without notice.

Entlassung *(f)* − dismissal, discharge, release, fristlose Entlassung: dismissal without notice; vorübergehende Entlassung: lay off.

Entlassungsabfindung *(f)* − severance pay.

Entlassungsentschädigung *(f)* − dismissal compensation, layoff benefit.

Entlassungsgeld *(n)* − severance wage, dismissal pay.

Entlassungsgrund *(m)* − reason/grounds *(Pl)* for discharge/dismissal.

Entlassungszeugnis *(n)* — certificate of discharge.

Entleiher *(m)* *(nach dem Arbeitnehmerüberlassungsgesetz)* — manpower supply client.

entlohnen — to pay off, to compensate ⟨AE⟩.

Entlohnung *(f)* — payment, pay, remuneration, compensation ⟨AE⟩.

Entlohnungsgrundsatz *(m)* — remuneration principle.

Entlohnungspflicht *(f)* — obligation to remunerate.

Entmündigung *(f)* — interdiction, disqualification, incapacitation.

Entschädigung *(f)* — compensation, indemnification, indemnity.

Entscheidungsfindung *(f)* — decision making.

Entschuldigung *(f)* — excuse, apology; schriftliche Entschuldigung: written justification/apology.

Entziehungskur *(f)* — dry-out, corrective training.

Erfindervergütung *(f)* — remuneration for employee-inventions.

Erfolgsbeteiligung *(f)* ⟨am Produktivitätszuwachs⟩ — progress sharing.

Erfolgslohn *(m)* — result wage, payment by results.

Ergänzungsabgabe *(f)* — surtax.

Ergonomie *(f)* — ergonomics *(PI)*.

Erholung *(f)* — recreation, relaxation: ⟨Arbeitsruhe⟩, vacation, holiday ⟨Ferien⟩, convalescence, recovery ⟨Krankheit⟩.

Erholungsbedarf *(m)* — rest period requirement.

Erholungskur *(f)* — rest cure.

Erholungspause *(f)* — rest period.

Erholungsprogramm *(n)* — recreational program(me).

Erholungsurlaub *(m)* — holiday, vacation ⟨AE⟩.

Erholungszuschlag *(m)* — fatigue allowance.

Erholzeit *(f)* — rest time.

erledigen — to execute, to finish, to settle, to fix up; Arbeitsrückstände erledigen: to clear off arrears of work.

Ermüdungszuschlag *(m)* — fatigue allowance.

ernennen — to appoint.

Ernennung *(f)* — appointment.

Ersatzbedarf *(m)* — replacement needs *(PI)*.

Ersatzbeschaffung *(f)* — replacement.

Ersatzeinstellung *(f)* — replacement.

Ersatzmitglied *(n)* — deputy member, substitute.

Erschöpfung *(f)* — exhaustion.

Erschöpfungszustand *(m)* — state of exhaustion.

Erschwernis *(n)* — handicap, impediment, aggravation.

Erschwerniszulage *(f)* — severity/ hardship allowance.

Erwerbsfähigkeit *(f)* — ability to earn a livelihood.

erwerbslos *(adj)* — unemployed, unoccupied, out of work, jobless ⟨AE⟩.

Erwerbslosenfürsorge *(f)* — unemployment relief.

Erwerbslosenunterstützung *(f)* — unemployment benefit; Erwerbslosenunterstützung beziehen: to be/to live on the dole ⟨BE⟩, to be on the unemployment rolls ⟨AE⟩.

erwerbstätig *(adj)* — gainfully employed.

erwerbsunfähig *(adj.)* — permanently disabled.

Erwerbsunfähigkeit *(f)* — disability, disablement, incapacity for employment; dauernde Erwerbsunfähigkeit: permanent disability; zeitweilige Erwerbsunfähigkeit: temporary disability.

Erziehungsbeihilfe *(f)* — education subsidy/allowance, educational grant.

Erziehungsurlaub *(m)* — educational leave.

Essenbon *(m)* / **Essenmarke** *(f)* — meal ticket/voucher, bread ticket ⟨AE⟩.

Essenspause *(f)* — meal break.

F

Fabrikarbeiter(in) *(m⟨f⟩)* — industrial worker/labo(u)rer, factory worker, operative.

Fabrikationseinrichtung *(f)* — production facilities, productive equipment.

Facharbeiter *(m)* — craftsman, skilled worker/operative, skilled labo(u)r.

Facharbeiterlohn *(m)* — occupational wage.

Fachausbildung *(f)* — occupational training, vocational training, professional training, special training.

Fachhochschule *(f)* — professional school.

Fachkenntnisse *(f, Pl)* — special knowledge; besondere Fachkenntnisse: know how.

Fachkraft *(f)* — skilled worker, qualified worker; Fachkraft für Arbeitssicherheit: (occupational) safety specialist.

Fachkräfte *(f, Pl)* — skilled labo(u)r, technical manpower.

Fachkunde *(f)* — professional knowledge.

fachlich *(adj)* — professional, functional.

Fachmann *(m)* — expert, specialist, profesional.

fachmännisch *(adj)* — professional, specialized.

Fachpersonal *(n)* — skilled staff/personnel, trained staff.

Fachschulbildung *(f)* — technical/professional training.

Fachzeitschrift *(f)* — business paper, professional magazine.

Fähigkeitsanforderung *(f)* — ability requirement.

Fahrgemeinschaft *(f)* — transportation pool.

Fahrtkosten *(Pl)* — travel(ling) expenses.

Fahrtkostenerstattung *(f)* — transportation cost refund.

Fahrtkostenzuschuß *(m)* — transportation/travel allowance.

Familienbeihilfe *(f)* — family allowance.

Familienfürsorge *(f)* — family care.

Familienstand *(m)* — marital status.

faul *(adj)* — lazy, idle.

faulenzen — to loaf, to be on the loaf.

Faulenzer *(m)* — loafer, shuggard.

fehlen — to be absent; unentschuldigt fehlen: to be absent without good excuse.

Feierabend *(m)* — leisure time.

Feierschicht *(f)* — scheduled shift off.

Feiertag *(m)* — holiday; allgemeiner Feiertag: public holiday; gesetzlicher Feiertag: legal holiday.

Feiertagsarbeit *(f)* — holiday work.

Feiertagslohnzahlungsgesetz *(n)* — Pay for Public Holidays Act ⟨= *Act respecting the payment of wages for public holidays*⟩.

Feiertagsvergütung *(f)* — holiday pay.

Feiertagszuschlag *(m)* — holiday premium.

Ferien *(Pl)* — holiday, vacation ⟨*AE*⟩.

Ferienarbeit *(f)* — holiday/vacation ⟨*AE*⟩ work.

Ferienbeschäftigung *(f)* — holiday/vacation ⟨*AE*⟩ post.

Ferienordung *(f)* — holiday/vacation ⟨*AE*⟩ schedule.

Ferienzeit *(f)* — holiday season, vacation period ⟨*AE*⟩.

Fernlehrgang *(m)* — correspondence course.

Fernlehrinstitut *(n)* — correspondence school/college.

Fertigmontage *(f)* — final assembly.

Fertigungskosten *(Pl)* — cost of production, production cost.

Fertigungslöhne *(m, Pl)* — direct labo(u)r cost, productive wages.

flexibel *(adj)* — flexible; flexible Altersgrenze: flexible age limit; flexible Arbeitszeit: flextime, flexible work(ing) time.

Fließband *(n)* — production/moving line, assembly line ⟨*Montageband*⟩.

Fließbandbesetzung *(f)* line manning.

Fließbandgeschwindigkeit *(f)* — (production/moving) line speed.

Fließbandfertigung *(f)* — (moving) line production.

Fluktuation *(f)* ⟨*von Arbeitskräften*⟩ — employee turnover, fluctuation.

Forderung *(f)* — claim, demand, request.

Forderungspaket *(n)* — package claim.

Förderung *(f)* — promotion, advancement; berufliche Förderung: career advancement.

Förderungsunterricht *(m)* — remedial instruction.

Fortbildung *(f)* — further/supplementary education/training, advanced training, improvement (of one's knowledge/training).

Fortbildungskurs(us) *(m)* / **Fortbildungslehrgang** *(m)* — adult education course, refresher course, continuation course.

Fragebogen *(m)* — questionnaire.

Frauenarbeit *(f)* — female occupation.

Frauenarbeitsschutz *(m)* — women's safety provisions *(Pl)*.

Freibetrag *(m)* — ⟨*bei der Steuer:*⟩ exempted amount ⟨*Steuer*⟩, ⟨*bei der Einkommensteuer:*⟩ income tax relief ⟨*BE*⟩: ⟨*Einkommensteuer*⟩, ⟨*bei der Lohnsteuer:*⟩ withholding exemption.

freisetzen ⟨*Arbeitskräfte*⟩ — to make idle, to lay off.

freistellen ⟨*von der Arbeit*⟩ — to give s. o. leave, to release s. o. from work.

Freistellung *(f)* ⟨*von der Arbeit*⟩ — release from work.

Freizeit *(f)* — leisure, sparetime, time off.

Freizeiteinrichtung *(f)* — recreation facility.

Freizeitgestaltungsprogramm *(n)* — leisure/recreation service.

Fremdarbeiter *(m)* — foreign worker/labo(u)r, immigrant worker.

Friedenspflicht *(f)* ⟨*der Tarifpartner*⟩ — obligation to keep peace.

Frühschicht *(f)* — morning shift.

führen — to lead, to conduct, to guide, to manage ⟨*leiten*⟩.

Führungseigenschaft *(f)* — leadership/managerial quality, executive ability.

Führungsbefugnis *(f)* — managerial authority.

Führungsebene *(f)* — managerial level.

Führungskraft *(f)* — manager, executive employee.

Führungsmethode *(f)* — mangerial techniques *(Pl)*.

Führungsnachwuchs *(m)* — prospective managers, management trainees.

Führungspersönlichkeit *(f)* — dominant leader.

Führungspotential *(n)* — leadership/management, potential.

Führungsqualitäten *(f, Pl)* — management skills.

Führungsspitze *(f)* — top management.

Führungsstil *(m)* — management style.

Führungszeugnis *(n)* — good conduct certificate, certificate of character.

Funktion *(f)* — function.

Funktionsbeschreibung *(f)* — statement of functions.

Funktionszulage *(f)* — special allowance.

Fürsorge *(f)* — social service/welfare, care.

Fürsorgeempfänger *(m)* — welfare recipient.

Fürsorgeleistungen *(f, Pl)* — welfare benefits.

Fürsorgepflicht *(f)* ⟨*des Arbeitgebers*⟩ — employer's duty for social care, obligation to provide welfare.

G

Ganztagsbeschäftigung *(f)* — full-time employment/job.

Gastarbeiter *(m)* — immigrant worker ⟨*Fremdarbeiter*⟩, migrant labo(u)r.

Gebrechlichkeit *(f)* — invalidity, disability.

Geburtenbeihilfe *(f)* — maternity benefit.

Gedinge *(n)* — piecework, contract system; im Gedinge arbeiten: to work by the job.

Gefährdungshaftung *(f)* — strict/absolute liability.

Gefahrenzulage *(f)* — hazard bonus, danger allowance.

gegenseitig *(adj)* — mutual, reciprocal.

Gehalt *(n)* — salary; volles Gehalt: full salary.

Gehaltsabrechnung *(f)* — salary slip, ⟨*der Vorgang der Gehaltsabrechnung:*⟩ payroll.

Gehaltsangleichung *(f)* — salary adjustment.

Gehaltsempfänger *(m)* — salaried employee.

Gehaltsentwicklung *(f)* ⟨*persönliche*⟩ — salary history.

Gehaltserhöhung *(f)* — salary increase, salary advance, rise in pay/salary ⟨*colloq*⟩.

Gehaltsfortzahlung *(f)* ⟨*im Krankheitsfall*⟩ — continued payment during illness.

Gehaltsgruppe *(f)* — salary grade.

Gehaltskonto *(n)* — salary account.

Gehaltsliste *(f)* — salary role, pay sheet, salaries list.

Gehaltsstreifen *(m)* — salary slip.

Gehaltstabelle *(f)* — salary scale, pay schedule.

Gehaltsverwaltung *(f)* — salary administration.

Gehaltszulage *(f)* — extra pay, salary bonus.

Gehilfe *(m)* — journeyman, assistant, aid.

gekündigt sein — to be under notice to quit.

gekündigt werden — to receive one's notice, to be fired *⟨AE⟩*, to get sacked: *⟨colloq.⟩*.

Geldfaktor — cash coefficient *⟨= price per time unit⟩*.

Geldüberweisung *(f)* — money transfer, transmission of money.

Gelegenheitsarbeit *(f)* — occasional work.

Geltungsbereich *(m)* — area of competence, coverage.

Gemeinkosten *(Pl)* — overhead, fixed costs.

Gemeinkostenanteil *(m)* — overhead rate.

gemeinnützig *(adj)* — charitable, non-profit-making.

Gemeinschaftsarbeit *(f)* — teamwork.

Gemeinschaftsküche *(f)* — canteen.

Gemeinschaftsraum *(m)* — recreation room.

Generalstreik *(m)* — general/mass strike.

Generalvollmacht *(f)* — general authority/power.

Genesungsurlaub *(m)* — convalescent leave.

Gesamtbelegschaft *(f)* — total workforce.

Gesamtbetriebsrat *(m)* — central works council.

Gesamteinkommen *(n)* — total income/revenue.

Gesamtheit *(f)* *⟨der Beschäftigten⟩* — overall employment.

Gesamtleistung *(f)* — overall efficiency, total output.

Gesamtprokura *(f)* — joint signature.

Gesamtschule *(f)* — comprehensive school *⟨BE⟩*.

Gesamtverdienst *(m)* — total earnings.

Gesamtvereinbarung *(f)* — collective agreement.

Gesamtvergütung *(f)* — compensation package.

geschäftlich *(adj)* — commercial, on business; geschäftlich tätig sein: to be in business; geschäftlich unterwegs sein: to travel on business.

Geschäftsbereich *(m)* — function, area of operation, sphere of business.

Geschäftsbericht *(m)* — business report.

geschäftsfähig *(adj)* — legally competent/responsible, having legal capacity to make contracts; voll geschäftsfähig: having full (legal) capacity, to be fully capable; beschränkt geschäftsfähig: having restricted (legal) capacity.

Geschäftsfähigkeit *(f)* — full legal age (for), legal capacity, capacity to act; beschränkte Geschäftsfähigkeit: restricted capacity to contract.

geschäftsführend *(adj)* — acting, managing; geschäftsführender Gesellschafter: managing partner.

Geschäftsgeheimnis *(n)* – business secret.

Geschäftsreise *(f)* – business trip/travel.

Geschäftsverteilungsplan *(m)* – organizing chart.

Geselle *(m)* – journeyman.

Gesellenbrief *(m)* – certificate of apprenticeship.

Gesellenprüfung *(f)* – journeyman's/apprentices' (final) examination.

Gesellin *(f)* – trained woman, journeywoman.

Gesetzesverstoß *(m)* – law breaking, violation of the law, offence ⟨BE⟩, offense ⟨AE⟩.

Gesetzgebung *(f)* – legislation; arbeitsrechtliche Gesetzgebung: labo(u)r legislation.

gesetzlich *(adj)* – legal ⟨gesetzlich zulässig⟩, legitimate ⟨mit berechtigtem Anspruch auf⟩, statutory ⟨gesetzlich vorgeschrieben⟩, lawful ⟨dem Gesetz entsprechend, gesetzlich zulässig⟩.

gesetzlich *(adv)* – legally, lawfully, by law, according to law.

gesetzwidrig *(adj)* – illegal, unlawful.

Gestaltung *(f)* design; ergonomische Gestaltung: ergonomic des ign.

Gesundheit *(f)* – health.

Gesundheitsattest *(n)* – health certificate.

Gesundheitsdienst *(m)* – health/medical service.

gesundheitsgefährdend *(adj)* – injurious to health.

Gesundheitsgefahr *(f)* – health hazard.

Gesundheitsnachweis *(m)* – health certificate.

Gesundheitsfürsorge *(f)* – health care.

Gesundheitsschäden *(m, Pl)* – health hazards, injury/damage to s. one's health.

gesundheitsschädlich *(adj)* / **gesundheitsschädigend** *(adj)* – injurious/detrimental to health, harmful, unhealthy, ⟨Klima, Nahrung:⟩ unwholesome, ⟨Gas, etc.:⟩ noxiuos, ⟨Verhältnisse:⟩ insanitary.

Gesundheitsschutz *(m)* – protection of health.

Gewerbeaufsichtsamt *(n)* / **Gewerbeaufsichtsbehörde** *(f)* – industrial inspection office/board, trade control office.

Gewerbeordnung *(f)*/**Gewerberecht** *(n)* – Trade Act, Industrial Code, trade regulations ⟨Pl⟩.

Gewerbetätigkeit *(f)* – industrial employment, industrial/gainful activity, trade.

Gewerbeunfallversicherung *(f)* – industrial insurance.

Gewerkschaft *(f)* – (trade) union, labor union ⟨AE⟩; die Gewerkschaften: organized labo(u)r ⟨Sg⟩.

gewerkschaftlich *(adv)* – unionized ⟨gewerkschaftlich organisiert⟩; sich gewerkschaftlich organisieren: to unionize, organize (o. s.) into a union, to form a (trade/labo(u)r) union; nicht gewerkschaftlich organisiert: unorganized, not unionized.

Gewerkschaft(l)er *(m)* – (trade) unionist, member of a (trade/labo(u)r) union, union member.

Gewerkschaftsbeitrag *(m)* – union due.

Gewerkschaftsbund *(m)* – federation of trade unions.

gewerkschaftsfeindlich *(adj)* — anti-union.

Gewerkschaftsfunktionär *(m)* — union official/officer, walking delegate ⟨*AE*⟩.

Gewerkschaftsverband *(m)* — Federation of Trade/Labo(u)r Unions.

Gewinnbeteiligung *(f)* — profit sharing, share in profits.

Gewohnheitsrecht *(n)* — general customs, customary right.

Glaubhaftmachung *(f)* — substantiation, satisfactory proof.

Gleichberechtigung *(f)* — equal rights (for women), equality of rights/status, concurrence ⟨*jur*⟩.

Gleichbehandlung *(f)* — equal treatment.

Gleichbehandlungsgrundsatz *(m)* — principle of equal treatment.

gleichberechtigt *(adj)* — having equal rights.

gleichgestellt *(adj)* — treated as equal.

Gleichgestellte(r) *(f, m)* — person placed on the same footing as severely handicapped persons.

Gleitzeit *(f)* — gliding time, flexible working hours.

Grad *(m)* — degree, grade, step ⟨*Rang*⟩, rank; akademischer Grad: academic degree/rank, university degree; akademischen Grad erlangen: to take/to make a degree.

Graphologie *(f)* — graphology.

Gratifikation *(f)* — bonus, gratuity.

Grenzgänger *(m)* — frontier worker.

grob *(adj)* — ⟨*Arbeit:*⟩ rough; grob fahrlässig: grossly negligent.

Großaktionär *(m)* — principal shareholder/stockholder ⟨*AE*⟩.

Großbetrieb *(m)* — large establishment, large-scale enterprise.

Großhandelskaufmann *(m)* — wholesaler, wholesale merchant.

Großraumbüro *(n)* — open-plan office.

Grubenarbeiter *(m)* — miner, pitman.

Grubensicherheit *(f)* — mine safety.

Grundausbildung *(f)* — basic training.

Grundeinkommen *(n)* — basic income.

Grundfertigkeiten *(f, Pl)* — basic skills.

Grundgehalt *(n)* — base salary.

Grundgesetz *(n)* — Constitution, Basic Law for the Federal Republic of Germany.

Grundlohn *(m)* — basis wage(s), flat rate, base wage, base rate.

Grundrecht *(n)* — basic/constitutional right eines Bürgers.

Grundrente *(f)* — ground/annual/true rent, primary insurance amount.

Grundsatz *(m)* — principle, rule/policy; Grundsatz von Treu und Glauben: expectation of good faith.

Grundschul(aus)bildung *(f)* — primary/elementary education.

Grundstudium *(n)* — basic study.

Grundvergütung *(f)* — base/basic rate.

Gruppenakkord *(m)* — group incentive, group piecework.

Gruppenakkordlohn *(m)* — group piece rate.

Gruppenarbeit *(f)* — teamwork, bandwork.

Gruppendynamik *(f)* — group dynamics.

Gruppenlebensversicherung *(f)* — group-term life insurance.

Gruppenleistung *(f)* — group output.

Gruppenleiter(in) *(m⟨f⟩)* — group manager/supervisor.

Gültigkeit *(f)* — validity, effect, force;

Gültigkeit eines Vertrages: force of an agreement.

Gültigkeitsbereich *(m)* — range of validity, ⟨*eines Gesetzes:*⟩ scope.

Gültigkeitsdauer *(f)* — running/validation period.

Gutachten *(n)* — expert opinion, expertise survey, report; ärztliches Gutachten: medical certificate/opinion.

gutgläubig *(adj)* — ⟨*Kauf, Tat, etc.:*⟩ (done) in good faith, ⟨*Person:*⟩ (acting) in good faith, bona fide.

gütlich *(adj)* — amicable, voluntary; sich gütlich einigen: to settle amicably.

Gymnasialausbildung *(f)* — grammar-school education.

Gymnasiast(in) *(m⟨f⟩)* — grammar-school student.

Gymnasium *(n)* — grammar/public school ⟨*BE*⟩, high school ⟨*AE*⟩.

H

Hafenarbeiter *(m)* — docker ⟨(*BE*⟩, dock labour(er)/worker, longshoreman ⟨*AE*⟩.

Haft *(f)* — imprisonment, custody, detention, hold; in Haft: under arrest, in prison/custody, detained.

haftbar *(adj)* — responsible, (legally) liable; persönlich haftbar sein: to be personally answerable.

haften *(für)* — to be liable/answerable for, to respond ⟨*AE*⟩; für einen Schaden haften: to be (held) liable for a charge.

Haftpflicht *(f)* — liability, accountability, gesetzliche Haftpflicht: legal liability.

Haftpflichtversicherung *(f)* — liability/third-pary insurance.

Haftung *(f)* — liability, responsibility ⟨*Verantwortung*⟩, warranty, guarantee ⟨*Bürgschaft*⟩; persönliche Haftung: private liability; gesamtschuldnerische Haftung: joint and several liability; unmittelbare Haftung: primary liability; Gesellschaft mit beschränkter Haftung: private limited company.

halbtägig *(adj)*/**halbtags** *(adj)* — half-time, part time; nur halbtägig arbeiten: to work half-time.

Halbtagsarbeit *(f)* — part-time employment, half-day (-time) job.

Halbtagskraft *(f)* — part-time worker, half-timer, part-timer.

Halbtagsstelle *(f)* — part-time job.

Handarbeit *(f)* — handiwork, handwork, common/unskilled work, manual labo(u)r/work.

Handarbeiter *(m)* — manual worker, labo(u)rer, blue-collar worker ⟨*AE*⟩.

Handbuch *(n)* — handbook, manual.

Handeln *(n)* — doing, action, activity ⟨*Tätigkeit*⟩, trading ⟨*Handel treiben*⟩, fahrlässiges Handeln: active negligence.

Handelsakademie *(f)* — commercial/business ⟨*AE*⟩ school.

Handelsenglisch *(n)* — business English.

Handelsgericht *(n)* — commercial court.

Handelsgesetz *(n)* — commercial law.

Handelsgesetzbuch *(n)* — Code of Commerce, Commercial Code.

Handelskammer *(f)* — chamber of commerce, board ⟨*AE*⟩/court of trade;

Industrie- und Handelskammer: Chamber of Industry and Commerce, Internationale Handelskammer: International Chamber of Commerce.

Handelsrecht *(n)* — commercial law; Gesellschaften des Handelsrechts: companies under mercantile law.

handelsrechtlich *(adj)* — under/in accordance with commercial law.

Handelsregister *(n)* — trade register, commercial register; ins Handelsregister eintragen: to register ⟨BE⟩, to incorporate ⟨AE⟩.

Handelsreisender *(m)* — commercial travel(l)er.

Handelsschule *(f)* — commercial school/college.

Handelsvertreter *(m)* — commercial agent, sales agent.

Handfertigkeit *(f)* — manual skill, handicraft.

Handlungsgehilfe *(m)* — merchant's clerk.

Handlungsvollmacht *(f)* — authority to act, procuration ⟨Prokura⟩.

Handschrift *(f)* — handwriting.

Handschriftenprobe *(f)* — specimen of one's handwriting.

handschriftlich *(adj)* — handwritten, in writing.

Handwerker *(m)* — craftsman, handicraftsman, workman.

Handwerksbursche *(m)* — journeyman.

Handwerksmeister *(m)* — craftmaster, trademaster.

Härteausgleich *(m)* (bei Dienstentlassung) — severance pay, dismissal compensation.

Härteregelung *(f)* — settlement of hardship cases.

Hauptabteilung *(f)* — main department, central department.

hauptamtlich *(adj)* — full-time; hauptamtlich arbeiten: to work on full-time basis.

hauptberuflich *(adj)* — professional, as a regular occupation.

Haupterwerbszweig *(m)* — main profession.

Hauptfach *(n)* — speciality, ⟨in der Schule:⟩ special/main subject, major ⟨AE⟩; Hauptfach studieren: to major a subject ⟨AE⟩.

Hauptfürsorgestelle *(f)* — central/main assistance office.

Haupttätigkeit *(f)* — principal occupation.

Hauptverwaltung *(f)* — central office, headquarters, general administration.

Hauptversammlung *(f)* — general company meeting, general stockholder's meeting ⟨AE⟩.

Hauptvorstand *(m)* — governing board (of directors).

Hausangestellte *(f)* — (domestic) servant, maid (servant), ⟨AE⟩.

Hausarbeitstag *(m)* — woman's housework day, day off for women with own household.

Hausfrau *(f)* — housewife.

Haushälterin *(f)* — lady housekeeper.

Haushaltshilfe *(f)* — household/domestic help.

Haushaltungsschule *(f)* — domestic science college.

Haustarif *(m)* — company/direct union agreement.

Hauswirtschaftslehre *(f)* — domestic science.

Heer *(n)* — army, armed forces; im Heer dienen: to serve with the colo(u)rs.

Heilfürsorge *(f)* — sanitation.

Heimarbeit *(f)* —indoor work, outwork.

Heimarbeiter *(m)* — outworker, home-worker, taker-in.

Heimatanschrift *(f)* — home address.

Heimatort *(m)* — native place.

Heimaturlaub *(m)* — home leave.

Heiratsbeihilfe *(f)*/**Heiratszuschuß** *(m)* — marriage allowance.

Heiratsurkunde *(f)* — marriage certificate.

Hilfsarbeiter *(m)* — unskilled/auxiliary worker, help(er) ⟨*Aushilfe*⟩; wissenschaftlicher Hilfsarbeiter: unestablished assistant.

hilfsbedürftig *(adj)* — needy, in need of assistance.

Hilfsperson *(n)* — auxiliary personnel, ancillary workers, helpers.

Hilfsschule *(f)* — special school for educationally subnormal children.

Hinterbliebenenbezüge *(m, Pl)* — widow's benefit ⟨*BE*⟩.

Hinterbliebenenrente *(f)* — death benefit.

Hinterbliebenenversorgung *(f)* — survivors' benefit/pension.

hochbegabt *(adj)* — highly gifted.

Hochkonjunktur *(f)* — boom, high industrial activity, peak prosperity.

Hochschulabsolvent(in) *(m* ⟨*f*⟩*)* — (university) graduate.

Hochschulbildung *(f)* — university education.

Höchstalter *(n)* — maximum age.

Höchstarbeitszeit *(f)* — maximum working time, maximum time of work/employment.

Honorar *(n)* — remuneration, reward ⟨*Entlohnung*⟩, gratification ⟨*Belohnung*⟩, fee, honorarium; festes Honorar: salary compensation, general retainer; jmd. ein Honorar zahlen: to pay s. o. a fee.

hörgeschädigt *(adj)* — hearing impaired.

humanistische Bildung *(f)* — classical education.

Humanisierung *(f)* des Arbeitslebens — humanisation of work(ing) life.

Hungerlohn *(m)* — starvation wages, sweated money, pittancy, penny fee ⟨*BE*⟩.

I

Ideenfindung *(f)* — brainstorming.

Immobilienmanager *(m)* — real estate manager.

Immobilienverwalter *(m)* — property manager.

Impfschein *(m)* — vaccination certificate.

Indexlohn *(m)* — pegged wages.

Industrie *(f)* — (manufacturing) industry; in der Industrie beschäftigt: engaged in industry; eisenverarbeitende Industrie: ironworking industry; metallverarbeitende Industrie: metalworking industry; stahlverarbeitende Industrie: steel-using industry.

Industriearbeiter *(m)* — industrial worker/labo(u)r, factory worker.

Industrieberater *(m)* — industrial/management consultant.

Industrieerfahrung *(f)* — industrial experience.

Industriegelände *(n)* — industrial estate/area/park ⟨*AE*⟩.

Industriegewerkschaft *(f)* — industrial/ trade/labor union.

Industrieverband *(m)* — trade association, federation of industries.

Industrie- und Handelskammer *(f)* — Chamber of Industrie and Commerce.

Informationspflicht *(f)* *(des Arbeitgebers)* — obligation to inform the employees.

Informationsrecht *(n)* — right to information/be notified.

Initiative *(f)* — initiative, enterprise, pep, getup ⟨*AE*⟩; Initiative besitzen: to be enterprising, to have pep; Initiative vermissen lassen: to be lacking in drive.

innerbetrieblich *(adj)* — intercompany, in-plant ⟨*AE*⟩; innerbetriebliche Beziehungen: employe(e)/labo(u)r relations.

Inserat *(n)* — insertion, insert, advertisement, ad ⟨*AE*⟩; Inserat aufgeben: to put in an advertisement; durch Inserat suchen: to advertise for.

Insolvenzsicherung *(f)* — security against insolvency, protection of pensions in case of insolvency.

Instandhaltungspersonal *(n)* — maintenance employe(e)s.

Interessenausgleich *(m)* — reconciliation of interests.

Invalidenversicherungsbeitrag *(m)* — social security contribution.

Invalidität *(f)* — disablement, invalidity, permanent incapacity, disability ⟨*AE*⟩.

Invaliditätsrente *(f)* — disablement annuity.

J

Jahresabschlußvergütung *(f)* — year-end premium.

Jahreseinkommen *(n)* — annual income.

Jahreshauptversammlung *(f)* — annual general meeting.

Jahresurlaub *(m)* — annual holiday/ leave/vacation.

Jubilar(in) *(m* ⟨*f*⟩) — jubilarian.

Jubiläum *(n)* — anniversary, jubilee; Jubiläum begehen: to celebrate/to observe an anniversary.

Jubiläumsfeier *(f)* — celebration of jubilee.

Jugendarbeit *(f)* — work done by minors.

Jugendarbeitsschutzgesetz *(n)* — Young Persons Protection of Employment Act ⟨= *Act to protect young persons in employment*⟩.

Jugendpfleger *(m)* — child welfare worker.

Jugendversammlung *(f)* — juvenile employees' meeting.

Jugendvertretung *(f)* — representation of juvenile employees.

Junggeselle *(m)* — bachelor.

Junggesellenwohnung *(f)* — bachelor flat/quarters.

juristisch *(adj)* — legal, jurisdictial, jural.

K

Kammer *(f)* *(des Arbeitsgerichts)* — division of the labo(u)r court.

Kantine *(f)* — canteen, lunchroom ⟨*AE*⟩, commissary, cafeteria, ⟨*für Erfrischungen:*⟩ snack bar.

Kantineneinrichtung *(f)* — ⟨*Institution:*⟩ employe(e) food services, ⟨*Ausstattung:*⟩ canteen facilities.

Kantinenessen *(n)* — canteen food.

Kantinenwirt *(m)* — canteen manager.

Kapazität *(f)* — capacity, authority, expert ⟨*Fachmann*⟩; voll ausgenutzte Kapazität: full operating capacity; ungenützte Kapazität: idle/spare ⟨*BE*⟩ capacity; Kapazität voll ausnützen: to work to capacity.

kapitalstark *(adj)* — financially strong.

kaputt *(adj)* ⟨*colloq*⟩ — out of order, broken, packed up; sich kaputtarbeiten: to wear o. s. out; sich kaputtmachen: to fag o. s. out.

Karenzentschädigung *(f)* — compensation for competitive restriction.

Karenzzeit *(f)* — waiting/qualifying period.

Karriere *(f)* — career; Karriere machen: to make a career for o. s., to get ahed ⟨*AE*⟩; seiner Karriere schaden: to injure one's prospects.

Karrieremöglichkeiten *(f, Pl)* — career opportunities.

Karriereplanung *(f)* — career planning.

Kaufkraft *(f)* — ⟨*des Geldes:*⟩ purchasing power, ⟨*der Konsumenten:*⟩ spending power.

Kaufkraftausgleich *(m)* — purchasing-power allowance.

Kaufkraftparität *(f)* — purchasing-power parity.

kaufkräftig *(adj)* — ⟨*Währung:*⟩ having purchasing power, hard (currency), ⟨*Verbraucher:*⟩ able to buy, moneyed, well-to-do.

kaufmännisch *(adj)* — commercial, mecantile; kaufmännische(r) Angestellte(r): clerk; kaufmännische Lehre *(f)*: apprenticeship; kaufmännische(r) Auszubildende(r): apprentice.

Kaufmannsgehilfenprüfung *(f)* — business college/school examination.

Kernarbeitszeit *(f)* — core time.

Kettenarbeitsvertrag *(m)* — chain employment contract.

Kilometergeld *(n)* — mileage allowance.

Kilometerpauschale *(f)* — mileage rebate, lump-sum mileage allowance.

Kind *(n)* — child; eheliches Kind: legitimate child; uneheliches Kind: illegitimate child; minderjähriges Kind: infant, minor.

Kindergeld *(n)* — children's/family allowance.

Kinderzulage *(f)* — dependency bonus/allowance, children's allowance ⟨*BE*⟩, child bounty ⟨*AE*⟩.

Klage *(f)* — legal action, lawsuit, suit, complaint, grievance ⟨*Beschwerde*⟩; Klage auf Schadenersatz: damages suit; Klage wegen Vertragsverletzung: action for breach of contract.

Klempner *(m)* — plumber.

Knappschaftskasse *(f)* — miners' insurance, miners' provident/benefit fund.

Koalitionsbildung *(f)* − formation of a coalition.

Koalitionsfreiheit *(f)* − right to form unions and associations/coalitions, freedom of association.

Kollege *(m)* − colleague, fellow-worker.

Kollektivarbeitsvertrag *(m)* − collective labo(u)r agreement.

Kollektivvertrag *(m)* − collective agreement/contract.

Kollektiv(vertrags)verhandlungen *(f, Pl)* − collective bargaining.

Kolonnenführer *(m)* − group leader.

kompetent *(adj)* − competent, responsible, authoritative; kompetent sein: to be an expert/authority on a subjekt.

Konjunktur *(f)* − market prospects, state of the economy, economic trend, economic situation/activity ⟨*Wirtschaftslage*⟩, business outlook/trend, boom, peak prosperity, high industrial activity ⟨*Hochkonjunktur*⟩.

Konjunkturablauf *(m)* − economic trend.

Konjunkturabschwächung *(f)* − decline in/slackening of economic activity, downward movement, downswing, downward trend in the business cycle, recession.

Konjunkturkreislauf *(m)* − business/economic/trade cycle.

Konkurrenzklausel *(f)* − competition clause, restraint clause, stipulation in restraint of trade.

Konkurrenzverbot *(n)* − restraint of trade, exclusivity stipulation ⟨*BE*⟩.

Konkurs *(m)* − bankruptcy, insolvency, business failure; Konkurs anmelden: to file a petition in bancruptcy; Konkurs machen/in Konkurs gehen: to go/ to become bancrupt, to fail; Konkurs eröffnen: to institute bancruptcy proceedings.

Konkursausfallgeld *(n)* − payment in respect of wage debts in the event of bankruptcy.

Können *(n)* − ability, skill, faculty.

Konstrukteur *(m)* − design engineer, constructor.

kontaktfähig *(adj)* − sociable.

Konto *(n)* − account; Konto pfänden: to garnish, to attach ⟨*AE*⟩.

Konzernbetriebsrat *(m)* − combine works council.

körperbehindert *(adj)* − handicapped.

körperlich *(adj)* − physical, material, bodily; körperliche Arbeit: manual work/labo(u)r.

Körperschutzmittel *(n)* − personal protective equipment.

Kosten *(Pl)* − cost, costs, expense(s), charges, fees ⟨*Gebühren*⟩; Kosten einsparen: to cut back on costs.

Kostenabbau *(m)* − cost reduction, cost cut.

kostenbewußt *(adj)* − cost-conscious.

Kraftfahrer *(m)* − driver, automobilist.

Kraftfahrzeugschlosser *(m)* − automobile mechanic.

Krankenbeihilfe *(f)* − sickness allowance.

Krankengeld *(n)* − sickness benefit ⟨*BE*⟩, sickpay.

Krankenhausbeihilfe *(f)* − in-hospital benefit.

Krankenkasse *(f)* − sick-fund, sickness insurance fund/plan ⟨*AE*⟩, health insurance company/scheme/plan.

Krankenschwester *(f)* − (sick)nurse.

Krankenversicherung *(f)* − health insurance.

Krankenversicherungsbeitrag *(m)* − health insurance premium.

krankfeiern − to malinger, to swing the lead, to sham illness.

krankgeschrieben sein − to be on the sick list.

Krankheit *(f)* − illness, sickness.

krankheitsanfällig *(adj)* − prone to disease.

krankschreiben − to put on the sick list.

Kriegsbeschädigtenrente *(f)* − war pension.

Kriegsbeschädigung *(f)* − war disablement.

Kriegsdienstverweigerer *(m)* − resister, conscientious objector.

Kriegsdienstverweigerung *(f)* − conscientious objection.

kündbar *(adj)* − subject to notice: ⟨Anstellung, Miete⟩, terminable: ⟨Vertrag⟩, at call, callable, subject to call: ⟨Kapital⟩.

Kündbarkeit *(f)* − terminableness, liability to notice.

kündigen ⟨Arbeitgeber⟩ − to give notice to s. o., to give s. o. notice (of termination), to give notice (to terminate work), to terminate s. one's employment, mit einer Frist von X Monat(en) kündigen: give s. o. a X month's(s') notice; fristlos kündigen/entlassen: to dismiss s. o. without notice.

kündigen ⟨Arbeitnehmer⟩ − to sign off, to quit one's job.

Kündigung *(f)* − termination (of employment): notice (of termination), dismissal: ⟨Arbeitgeber⟩; fristlose Kündigung durch Arbeitnehmer: termination without notice; fristlose Kündigung durch Arbeitgeber: dismissal without notice; außerordentliche Kündigung: dismissal for exceptional reasons; ordentliche Kündigung: lawful/proper termination; sozial ungerechtfertigte Kündigung: socially unjustified dismissal; seine Kündigung einreichen: to give in one's notice.

Kündigungsabfindung *(f)* − severance/termination pay.

Kündigungsfrist *(f)* − notice period, term/period of termination; mit dreimonatiger Kündigungsfrist: subject to three months' notice; Kündigungsfrist einhalten: to observe a term of notice; auf Einhaltung der Kündigungsfrist verzichten: to waive notice; Ablauf der Kündigungsfrist: fulfillment of the notice period.

Kündigungsgrund *(m)* − reason/ground for giving notice.

Kündigungsklausel *(f)* − cancel(l)ation clause.

Kündigungsrecht *(n)* − right to give notice.

Kündigungsrücknahme *(f)* − withdrawal of termination.

Kündigungsschreiben *(n)* − (written) notice.

Kündigungsschutz *(m)* − protection against unwarranted notice/unlawful/dismissal.

Kündigungsschutzgesetz *(n)* − Protection Against Dismissal Act.

Kur *(f)* − cure, course of (medical) treatment.

Kurs *(m)* − course ⟨Lehrgang⟩, session ⟨Unterrichtsstunde⟩.

Kurzarbeit *(f)* − short time (work).

kurzarbeiten − to work short time.

Kurzarbeiter(in) *(m⟨f⟩)* − short-time worker, short-timer.

Kurzarbeitergeld *(n)* − short-time allowance.

Kurzarbeiterunterstützung *(f)* — shortened work-week allowance.

Kurzschrift *(f)* — shorthand, stenography; englische Kurzschrift beherrschen: to take English shorthand.

Kurzurlaub *(m)* — short leave.

L

Ladenschluß *(m)* — closing time.

Ladenschlußgesetz *(n)* — Law regulating the Closing of Shops.

Lagerarbeiter *(m)* — storeman, warehouse laborer ⟨AE⟩.

Lagerverwalter *(m)* — store-room clerk, warehouse keeper ⟨AE⟩.

Landesarbeitsamt *(n)* — Land Employment Office.

Landesarbeitsgericht *(n)* — Land Labo(u)r Court.

Langsamarbeiten *(n)* ⟨planmäßiges⟩ — go-slow ⟨BE⟩, work-to-rule ⟨BE⟩, work according to the book ⟨AE⟩.

Lärmschutz *(m)* — noise prevention.

Laufbahn *(f)* — career; berufliche Laufbahn: business career; Laufbahn einschlagen: to enter (upon) a career.

Laufzeit *(f)* — running period.

Laufzettel *(m)* — interoffice/routing slip.

Lebenshaltungskosten *(Pl)* — living costs, cost of living; gestiegene Lebenshaltungskosten: advanced/increased cost of living.

Lebenshaltungskosten — Ausgleich *(m)* — cost of living allowance ⟨„COLA"⟩.

Lebenslauf *(m)* ⟨geschriebener⟩ — curriculum vitae, personal history/record.

Lebensunterhalt *(m)* — livelihood, support, maintenance; seinen Lebensunterhalt verdienen: to earn one's living.

Lebensversicherung *(f)* — life insurance/assurance ⟨BE⟩.

Lebenswandel *(m)* — line of conduct, way of living; mit einwandfreiem Lebenswandel: clean-lived.

ledig *(adj)* — single, unmarried, sole.

Lehrberuf *(m)* — apprenticeable occupation, teaching job/profession.

Lehrbrief *(m)* — certificate of apprenticeship ⟨Zeugnis⟩, indenture, articles of apprenticeship ⟨Vertrag⟩; ⟨eines Fernlehrganges:⟩ correspondence lesson.

Lehre *(f)* — apprenticeship ⟨Ausbildung⟩, instruction, training ⟨Unterweisung⟩; in die Lehre gehen: to article, to indent(ure), to apprentice; zu jmd. in die Lehre kommen: to be apprenticed to s. o.; jmd. in die Lehre nehmen: to take s. o. as apprentice; in der Lehre sein: to be apprenticed, to serve one's articles.

Lehrgang *(m)* — training course.

Lehrgangsleiter *(m)* — training supervisor, chief instructor.

Lehrling *(m)* — apprentice, trainee, learner; kaufmännischer Lehrling: business trainee.

Lehrlingsausbildung *(f)* — training of apprentices.

Lehrmädchen *(n)* — (girl) apprentice.

Lehrvertrag *(m)* — indenture, articles of apprenticeship ⟨Pl⟩.

Lehrwerkstatt *(f)* — (apprentices') training shop, apprentice shop.

Lehrzeit *(f)* — (time of) apprenticeship; seine Lehrzeit ableisten: to serve one's time.

Lehrzeugnis *(n)* — apprentice's certificate.

Leiharbeitsverhältnis *(n)* — temporary employment on loan basis.

Leistung *(f)* — performance, work done, job ⟨*geleistete Arbeit*⟩, output, production ⟨*Erzeugung*⟩, efficiency, ability ⟨*Fähigkeit*⟩; nach Leistung bezahlt: paid by results; vertraglich geschuldete Leistung: contractual obligation; soziale Leistung: social contributions.

Leistungsabfall *(m)* — decline in performance.

Leistungsanreiz *(m)* — incentive.

Leistungsausgleich *(m)* — compensation for services (rendered).

leistungsbedingt *(adj)* — according to merit/productivity.

leistungsbezogene Lohn-/Gehaltserhöhung *(f)* — merit increase.

Leistungsbeurteilung *(f)* — performance report/appraisal/rating, efficiency rating.

Leistungsbewertung *(f)* — performance evaluation/rating, merit rating.

Leistungsbonus *(m)* — (merit) bonus, incentive pay/wage.

leistungsfähig *(adj)* — efficient, productive, solvent ⟨*zahlungsfähig*⟩, financially strong ⟨*kapitalstark*⟩, körperlich leistungsfähig: ablebodied.

Leistungsentgelt *(n)* — efficiency payments.

Leistungsfähigkeit *(f)* — efficiency, productivity, (production) capacity, output, solvency; berufliche Leistungsfähigkeit: job efficiency, körperliche Leistungsfähigkeit: physical capacity, finanzielle Leistungsfähigkeit: financial strength.

Leistungsgarantie *(f)* — performance guarantee/bond ⟨*AE*⟩.

Leistungsgrad *(m)* — performance/efficiency level.

Leistungsgradschätzung *(f)* — performance/efficiency rating.

Leistungslohn *(m)* — incentive pay/wages *(Pl)*, payment by results.

Leistungsmotivation *(f)* — achievement motivation.

Leistungsnorm *(f)* — standard of performance.

leistungspflichtig *(adj)* — liable for payment/services.

Leistungsprämie *(f)* — (merit) bonus, extra pay, premium pay ⟨*AE*⟩.

Leistungsprinzip *(n)* — performance principle.

leistungssteigernd *(adj)* — increasing efficiency/performance/output.

Leistungssteigerung *(f)* — increase in efficiency/performance.

Leistungssystem *(n)* — performance/efficiency system, piece-rate/piecework system ⟨*Akkord*⟩.

Leistungsverlust *(m)* — inefficiency.

Leistungswettbewerb *(m)* — efficiency contest.

Leistungszulage *(f)* — (merit) bonus, incentive pay/wage, piecework rate, performance allowance.

leiten — ⟨*Betrieb:*⟩ to run, to operate, to direct, to manage, to control, to superintendend ⟨*beaufsichtigen*⟩.

Leitender Angestellter *(m)* — managerial employee, manager.

Leiter *(m)* — manager, head, chief.

lernen — to learn, to study, to serve one's apprenticeship.

Leumund *(m)* — reputation, character, record; guter Leumund: good reputation; schlechter Leumund: bad record.

Leumundszeugnis *(n)* — certificate of good behavio(u)r/character, good-conduct certificate.

Lohn *(m)* — wage, pay(ment) ⟨*Bezahlung*⟩, earnings *(Pl)* ⟨*Verdienst*⟩, remuneration, compensation, emolument ⟨*Vergütung*⟩; auszuzahlender Lohn: take-home-pay; ortsüblicher Lohn: local wage; übertariflicher Lohn: out-of-line rate; vertraglich vereinbarter Lohn: contractual wage; Lohn einbehalten: to stop/to detain wages; Lohn kürzen: to cut down wages; Lohn pfänden: to garnishee/to attach ⟨*AE*⟩ the wages.

Lohn- und Gehaltssumme *(f)* — total of wages and salaries.

Lohn-/Gehaltsabzug *(m)* — payroll deduction.

Lohn-/Gehaltsgruppenumstufung *(f)* — re-classification.

Lohnabbau *(m)* — wage cut, reduction of wages/pay.

lohnabhängig *(adj)* — wage-dependant.

Lohnabhängige(r) *(m, f)* — wage earner, employee.

Lohnabkommen *(n)* / **Lohnabmachung** *(f)* — wage(s)/pay agreement.

Lohnabrechnung *(f)* — wage(s) statement, pay slip, payroll work ⟨*Vorgang*⟩.

Lohnabschlag *(m)* — payment on account.

Lohnabtretung *(f)* — wage assignment.

Lohnabzug *(m)* — deduction(s) from wages/pay.

Lohnangleichung *(f)* — wage adjustment.

Lohnanreiz *(m)* — wage incentive.

Lohnanspruch *(m)* — wage claim.

Lohnanstieg *(m)* — rise in wages, wage increase; allgemeiner Lohnanstieg: general increase.

Lohnanteil *(m)* — (share in) wages ⟨*Pl*⟩, portion of wage.

Lohnarbeit *(f)* — wage/paid labo(u)r.

Lohnarbeiter *(m)* — paid labo(u)rer, wage earner, wageworker ⟨*AE*⟩.

Lohnauftrieb *(m)* — upward tendency of wages, wage drift.

Lohnaufwand *(m)* — labo(u)r costs, wage costs.

Lohnausfall *(m)* — loss of wages/pay/earnings, wages/pay/earnings lost.

Lohnausfallvergütung *(f)* — compensation for wages/pay/earnings lost.

Lohnausgleich *(m)* — compensation for wage deficiencies, wage adjustment.

Lohnausgleichskasse *(f)* — wage equalisation fund.

Lohnauszahlung *(f)* — payment of wages.

Lohnbüro *(n)* — pay office, payroll department ⟨*AE*⟩.

Lohneingruppierung *(f)* — wage classification.

Lohneinkommen *(n)* — wage income.

Lohnempfänger(in) *(m⟨f⟩)* — wage earner, wageworker ⟨*AE*⟩, hourly paid employee.

Lohnentwicklung *(f)* — development of wages/pay.

Lohnerhöhung *(f)* — pay increase/increment/rise/raise ⟨*AE*⟩, wage increase/increment/rise/raise ⟨*AE*⟩; rückwirkende Lohnerhöhung: retroactive pay.

Lohnfestsetzung *(f)* — wage/pay fixing, wage determination, wage/rate setting.

Lohnforderung *(f)* — wage claim/demand.

Lohnfortzahlung *(f)* — continuation of payments (to sick workers).

Lohngefälle *(n)* — wage differential.

Lohngefüge *(n)* — wage/pay structure.

Lohngleichheit *(f)* — equality of pay, equality in/of wages.

Lohngleitklausel *(f)* — escalator clause.

Lohngruppe *(f)* — wage group/bracket/grade.

Lohnindex *(m)* — wage index.

Lohnkampf *(m)* — wage/pay dispute.

Lohnkommission *(f)* wage-control(l)ing committee.

Lohnkonflikt *(m)* — wage dispute/conflict.

Lohnkonto *(n)* — payroll/wage account.

Lohnkosten *(Pl)* — wage/labo(u)r costs.

Lohnkostenverteilung *(f)* — distribution of wage costs.

Lohnkurve *(f)* — wage(s) graph/curve.

Lohnkürzung *(f)* — wage(s)/pay cut, cut in wages/pay.

Lohnliste *(f)* — payroll (sheet), pay bill (sheet).

Lohnnachzahlung *(f)* — retroactive payment of wages.

Lohnnebenleistungen *(f, Pl)* — fringe benefits ⟨AE⟩.

Lohnniveau *(n)* — wage/pay/earnings level.

Lohnparität *(f)* — parity of wages.

Lohnpause *(f)* — pay pause.

Lohnpfändung *(f)* — garnishment of wages, wage attachement.

Lohnpolitik *(f)* — wage policy.

Lohnrate *(f)* — wage rate.

Lohnrechnung *(f)* — payroll bookkeeping/accounting, wage cost accounting.

Lohnrunde *(f)* — round of wage negotiations.

Lohnsatz *(m)* — wage rate.

Lohnsenkung *(f)* — wage(s)/pay cut, cut in wages/pay.

Lohnsicherung *(f)* — wage protection.

Lohnskala *(f)* — wage/pay scale; gleitende Lohnskala: sliding wage/pay scale.

Lohnspanne *(f)* — range of wage(s).

Lohnstaffelung *(f)* — differentiation/grading of wage(s).

Lohnsteuer *(f)* — withholding tax, employment tax ⟨AE⟩, wage(s) tax.

Lohnsteuerabzug *(m)* — deduction of wage(s) tax.

Lohnsteuerfreibetrag *(m)* — employee's withholding exemption.

Lohnsteuerjahresausgleich *(m)* — annual adjustment of income tax.

Lohnsteuerkarte *(f)* — wage(s) tax card/sheet, withholding statement ⟨AE⟩.

Lohnsteuerrückvergütung *(f)* — wage(s) tax refund.

Lohnstopp *(m)* — wage stop/freeze.

Lohnstreifen *(m)* — wage/pay slip.

Lohnstruktur *(f)* — wage structure.

Lohnstufe *(f)* — wage scale, wage group/grade.

Lohnsumme *(f)* — wage/payroll total, total wages ⟨Pl⟩.

Lohnsummensteuer *(f)* — tax on the total of wages and salaries paid, payroll tax ⟨AE⟩, selective employment tax ⟨BE⟩.

Lohntabelle *(f)* — pay/wage schedule.

Lohntag *(m)* — payday.

Lohntarif *(m)* — wage rate/scale.

Lohntüte *(f)* — pay packet.

Löhnung *(f)* — payment (of wages).

Löhnungstag *(m)* — payday.

Lohnvereinbarung *(f)* — wage/pay agreement.

Lohnverhandlungen *(f, Pl)* — wage(s) collective bargaining.

Lohnverwaltung *(f)* – wage administration.

Lohnvorschuß *(m)* – wage(s) advance.

Lohnzahlung *(f)* – payment (of wage(s)).

Lohnzettel *(m)* – pay/wage slip.

Lohnzulage *(f)* – wage increase/supplement, supplementary wage, raise ⟨*AE*⟩.

Lohnzuschlag *(m)* – extra pay.

M

Mangel *(m)* – ⟨*Knappheit:*⟩ shortage, scarcity, need; Mangel an Arbeitskräften: manpower shortage; Mangel an Arbeitskräften haben: to be shorthanded.

Mangelberuf *(m)* – scarce job.

Mankohaftung *(f)* – liability for deficit/deficiency.

Manteltarifvertrag *(m)* – employment conditions agreement, collective framework agreement.

Maschinenarbeiter *(m)* – machine/engine fitter, machinist, shopworker ⟨*AE*⟩.

Maschinenbauingenieur *(m)* – mechanical engineer.

Maßregelung *(f)* – disciplinary punishment, reprimand, crackdown ⟨*AE*⟩.

Maßregelungsverbot *(n)* – inhibition of disciplinary judgement.

Massenarbeitslosigkeit *(f)* – mass unemployment.

Massenentlassung *(f)* – mass release/dismissals ⟨*PI*⟩.

Mechaniker *(m)* – mechanic, operative, repairman ⟨*Auto, Flugzeug*⟩.

Mehrarbeit *(f)* – additional/extra work, overtime ⟨*Überstunden*⟩.

Mehrarbeitsstop *(m)* – overtime ban.

Mehrarbeitsvergütung *(f)* – overtime pay(ment).

Mehrarbeitszuschlag *(m)* – overtime premium.

Mehrbelastung *(f)* – extra charge/burden, overcharge, overload ⟨*Überlastung*⟩.

Mehrheitswahl *(f)* – majority vote.

Mehrleistung *(f)* – increased performance/efficiency.

Mehrschichtbetrieb *(m)* – multiple shift operation.

mehrsprachig *(adj)* – multilingual.

Meinungsbefragung *(f)* – opinion poll/research.

Meister *(m)* – foreman ⟨*Betriebsmeister*⟩, master (of a trade).

Meisterbrief *(m)* – master craftsman's certificate.

Meisterin *(f)* – forelady, forewoman ⟨*Betriebsmeisterin*⟩.

Meisterprüfung *(f)* – examination for the master's diploma/certificate.

Meldepflicht *(f)* – duty of notification.

meldepflichtig *(adj)* – ⟨*Krankheiten:*⟩ notifiable, subject to registration.

Mengenleistung *(f)* – output, productive/production capacity.

Mensch *(m)* – human being, man, individual, person; arbeitsscheuer Mensch: shirker; intelligenter Mensch: intellectual person.

Mietvertrag *(m)* – lease (contract).

Mietwohnung *(f)* – lodgings, lodgement, quarters, flat ⟨*BE*⟩, apartment ⟨*AE*⟩.

Mietzulage *(f)* — lodging allowance.

Mietzuschuß *(m)* — rent allowance.

Militärdienst *(m)* — military duty, active service, national service ⟨*BE*⟩.

Minderheiten *(f, Pl)* — minority groups.

Minderheitenschutz *(m)* — protection of minorities.

Minderleistung *(f)* — reduced output.

Mindestarbeitsbedingungen *(f, Pl)* — minimum employment conditions.

Mindestbeschäftigungszeit *(f)* — minimum period of employment.

Mindesteinkommen *(n)* — minimum income.

Mindestlohn *(m)* — minimum wage (rate).

Mitarbeit *(f)* — cooperation, assistance, collaboration; freie Mitarbeit: free-lance employment; unter Mitarbeit von: in cooperation/collaboration with; langjährige Mitarbeit bei: many years of working with.

mitarbeiten *(an, bei)* — to collaborate *(on)*, to join/to take part in the work, to assist; an einer Sache mitarbeiten: to collaborate in work on s. th.

Mitarbeiter(in) *(m⟨f⟩)* — ⟨*Betriebsangehörige(r):*⟩ staff member, employee, ⟨*Arbeitskollege:*⟩ colleague, co-worker, fellow-worker; freiberuflicher Mitarbeiter: free-lance contributor.

mitbestimmen — ⟨*im Betrieb:*⟩ to participate in the management, to co-determine.

Mitbestimmung *(f)* — co-determination, co-decision, co management, worker-participation.

Mitbestimmungsgesetz *(n)* — Co-determination Act.

Mitbestimmungsrecht *(n)* — right of co-determination.

Montan-Mitbestimmungsgesetz *(n)* — Co-management Act ⟨= *Act respecting co-management by employees in the boards of supervision and managing boards of undertakings in the mining industry and in the iron and steel production industry*⟩.

mitbeteiligen — to give s. o. a share/say (in s. th.).

Mitbewerber *(m)* — competitor, rival.

Mitglied *(n)* member; hinzugewähltes Mitglied: co-optee; stellvertretendes Mitglied: deputy member.

Mittagspause *(f)* — lunch break.

Mitwirkung *(f)* — participation, assistance, cooperation.

Mobilität *(f)* — mobility.

Montagearbeit *(f)* — assembly work.

Montagebetrieb *(m)* — assembly operation/shop.

Montanindustrie *(f)* — mining ⟨*coal, iron and steel*⟩ industry.

Musterung *(f)* ⟨*mil.*⟩ — recruitment, call-up.

Mutterschaft *(f)* — maternity, motherhood.

Mutterschaftsurlaub *(m)* — maternity leave.

Mutterschutz *(m)* — maternity protection, protection of mothers.

Mutterschutzgesetz *(n)* — Maternity Protection Act ⟨= *Law protecting mothers-to-be and nursing mothers*⟩.

N

Nacharbeit *(f)* — make-up-work.

Nachholtag *(m)* / **Vorholtag** *(m)* — make-up-day.

Nachtarbeit *(f)* — nightwork, work at night.

Nachtarbeitszuschlag *(m)* — nightwork premium.

Nachtschicht *(f)* — night shift; Nachtschicht haben: to be on night-shift.

Nachtschichtzulage *(f)* — night shift premium.

Nachuntersuchung *(f)* — re-examination.

Nachwuchskraft *(f)* — (management) trainee ⟨AE⟩.

Nachzahlung *(f)* — subsequent/supplementary payment.

Naturallohn *(m)* — wage(s) in kind.

Nebenabrede *(f)* — secondary agreement.

Nebenberuf *(m)* — avocation, sideline (employment), minor occupation.

nebenberuflich *(adj)* — avocational, as a secondary occupation, sideline.

Nebenbetrieb *(m)* — ancillary establishment.

Nebeneinkünfte *(f, Pl)* — emoluments, additional/supplementary income, perquisites ⟨BE⟩.

Nebentätigkeit *(f)* — sideline, subsidiary activity.

Nettobetrag *(m)* — net amount.

Nettoeinkommen *(n)* — net income.

Nettoeinnahme *(f)* — net proceeds/receipts/takings ⟨Pl⟩.

Nettogewinn *(m)* — net gain(s), net/clear profit.

Nettolohn *(m)* — net wages ⟨Pl⟩, take-home pay.

Nettolohnvereinbarung *(f)* — net wages agreement.

Nettoverdienst *(m)* — take-net pay, net income/salary/earnings ⟨Pl⟩, net pay, take-home pay.

Neubewertung *(f)* — re-classification.

nichtig *(adj)* — void.

Nichtigkeit *(f) (jur)* — voidness, nullity.

niederlegen — sein Amt niederlegen: to retire from office; Arbeit niederlegen: to (lay) down tools, to stop working.

Niedriglohn *(m)* — bottom pay rate.

Normalarbeitstag *(m)* — standard working day.

Normalarbeitszeit *(f)* — standard working time, base time.

Normaleinkommen *(n)* — straight income.

Normalleistung *(f)* — standard output, normal performance.

Normallohn *(m)* — regular pay/wage.

Notdienst *(m)* — emergency service.

Notunterkunft *(f)* — shelter.

O

Oberingenieur *(m)* — chief engineer.

Oberinspektor *(m)* — inspector general.

Oberlandesgericht *(n)* — Regional Court of Appeal.

Obmann *(m)* ⟨*im Betrieb*⟩ — shop steward.

Offenbarungspflicht *(f)* — obligation to disclose.

Ordnung *(f)* des Betriebes — order of the establishment/firm.

Organisationsplan *(m)* — organization chart.

Ortsklassenausgleich *(m)* — intercity (wage) differential.

Ortszuschlag *(m)* — residential allowance.

P

paritätisch besetzt *(adj)* — in equal number, in parity.

parteipolitische Betätigung *(f)* — party-political activity.

Pauschalabfindung *(f)* — lump-sum/over-all compensation.

Pauschale *(f)* — lump-sum, global amount, flat charge (rate).

Pauschalentschädigung *(f)* — lump-sum settlement.

Pauschalzahlung *(f)* — lump-sum payment, composition payment ⟨*Ablösung*⟩.

Pause *(f)* — rest ⟨*Ruhepause*⟩, break, recess ⟨*AE*⟩ ⟨*Arbeitspause*⟩.

Pausenraum *(m)* — break-room, rest room.

pendeln ⟨*zwischen Wohnort und Arbeitsplatz*⟩ — to commute.

Pendler *(m)* — daily breader ⟨*BE*⟩, commuter ⟨*AE*⟩.

Pendlerbus *(m)* — shuttle bus.

Pension *(f)* — retirement ⟨*Ruhestand*⟩, (old-age) pension, superannuation, retirement allowance; in Pension gehen: to retire; in Pension sein: to be retired, to be/to live in retirement; eine Pension beziehen: to draw a pension; mit Pension verabschiedet: pensioned-off.

Pensionär(in) *(m*⟨*f*⟩*)* — pensionary, pensioner, retiree.

pensionieren — to pension (off), to retire, to superannuate; sich pensionieren lassen: to retire (on a pension).

pensioniert *(adj)* — in retirement, pensioned-off.

Pensionierung *(f)* — retirement, retiring; Pensionierung wegen Erreichen der Altersgrenze: superannuation; vorzeitige Pensionierung: early retirement; zur Pensionierung anstehen: to qualify for a pension.

Pensionsalter *(n)* — retirement/retiring/pension (able) age.

Pensionsanspruch *(m)* — right/entitlement to a pension.

Pensionsbeitrag *(m)* — contribution to the pension scheme.

pensionsberechtigt *(adj)* — pensionable, entitled to/eligible for a pension.

Pensionsberechtigte(r) *(f⟨m⟩)* — person entitled to/eligible for a pension.

Pensionsberechtigung *(f)* — right/entitlement to a pension.

Pensionsempfänger(in) *(m⟨f⟩)* — pensionary, pensioner, retiree.

Pensionsfond *(m)* — pension/retirement/superannuation fund.

Pensionskasse *(f)* — pension/retirement/superannuation fund.

Pensionsplan *(m)* — pension plan.

pensionsreif *(adj)* — due for retirement: *⟨colloq⟩*.

Pensionsrückstellung *(f)* — pension reserve.

Pensionszusage *(f)* — pension pledge.

Personal *(n)* — personnel, staff, employees.

Personalabbau *(m)* — personnel/staff reduction, redundancy.

Personalabteilung *(f)* — personnel department/division, personnel office.

Personalakte *(f)* — personnel record/file.

Personalangaben *(f, Pl)* — personal data, personalia.

Personalangelegenheiten *(f, Pl)* — personnel matters/affairs.

Personalaufwendungen *—(f, Pl)* — personnel expenses.

Personalauswahl *(f)* — personnel selection.

Personalbedarf *(m)* — manpower/personnel requirement.

Personalbeschaffung *(f)* — recruitment *⟨AE⟩*.

Personalbestand *(m)* — (number of) personnel.

Personalbüro *(n)* — personnel office.

Personalchef *(m)* — personnel/staff manager, personnel/staff director, chief of personnel.

Personalfragebogen *(m)* — personnel questionnaire.

Personalführung *(f)* — personnel management.

personalintensiv *(adj)* — personnel-intensive.

Personalkartei *(f)* — personnel index.

Personalkosten *(Pl)* — personnel expenditure *(Sg)*.

Personalleiter *(m)* — personnel/staff manager, personnel/staff director.

Personalmangel *(m)* — shortage of personnel, manpower shortage; an Personalmangel leiden: to be understaffed.

Personalplanung *(f)* — *⟨quantitativ:⟩* manpower/personnel planning, *⟨qualitativ:⟩*, career planning.

Personalpolitik *(f)* — personnel policy.

Personalsachbearbeiter(in) *(m⟨f⟩)* — personnel officer.

Personalstärke *(f)* — headcount, personnel strength.

Personalstatut *(n)* — staff regulations *(Pl)*.

Personalunterlagen *(f, Pl)* — personnel records.

Personalvertretung *(f)* — representation of the personnel/staff.

Personalverwaltung *(f)* — personnel administration.

Personalverzeichnis *(n)* — staff list, list/register of employe(e)s.

Personalwechsel *(m)* — turnover/change/shift in the personnel/staff.

Personensicherungsgerät *(n)* — personal protection device.

Persönlichkeitsrecht *(n)* — personal/individual right.

Pfändung *(f)* — attachment, distrainment, distress, levy.

Pfändungsfreibetrag *(m)* — exempted amount.

Pfändungs- und Überweisungsbeschluß *(m)* — decree of forthcoming writ of attachment.

Pfleger *(m)* ⟨*für Entmündigte*⟩ — curator.

Pflicht *(f)* — duty, office, business, job ⟨*Amt*⟩, obligation/liability ⟨*Verpflichtung*⟩.

Pflichtplatz *(m)* — post reserved for severely handicapped persons.

Pflichtverletzung *(f)* — breach of duty, lapse from one's duty.

Pförtner *(m)* — gatekeeper, porter, doorkeeper.

Position *(f)* — position, post, job.

Posten *(m)* — post, position, job ⟨*Stellung*⟩; unbesetzter Posten: unfilled post, vacancy; jmd. für einen Posten bestimmen: to appoint s. o. to a post; sich um einen Posten bewerben: to run for a position.

Praktikant(in) *(m⟨f⟩)* — person undergoing practical training, (industrial) trainee.

Praktikum *(n)* — practical training (course), practical: ⟨*colloq*⟩; sein Praktikum machen/absolvieren: to do one's practical (training).

Prämie *(f)* — premium, reward ⟨*Belohnung*⟩, prize, award ⟨*Auszeichnung*⟩, bonus ⟨*Dividende, Gratifikation*⟩; Prämie im betrieblichen Vorschlagwesen: suggestion (program) award.

Prämienlohn *(m)* — premium/incentive pay.

Prämiensystem *(n)* — incentive pay/premium/bonus system.

prämi(i)eren — to award a prize to s. o., to award a bonus/premium for, **prämiiert**: prize-winning.

Prämiierung *(f)* — (presentation of a) prize/award.

Privatunterricht *(m)* — private lessons.

Probearbeitsverhältnis *(n)* — employment on trial basis, probationary employment.

Probezeit *(f)* — trial period, (time of) probation, qualifying period, probationary term; nach einer Probezeit von x Monaten: at the end of x months' probation; jmd. auf Probezeit einstellen: to take s. o. on trial.

Produktion *(f)* — production, output, manufacture; Produktion stillegen: to halt production lines.

Produktionsanlage *(f)* — production plant/facilities ⟨*Pl*⟩.

Produktionsanstieg *(m)* — increase in production/output.

Produktionsarbeiter(in) *(m⟨f⟩)* — production worker.

Produktionsausfall *(m)* — loss of production.

Produktionsausweitung *(f)* — expansion of production.

Produktionsbereich *(m)* — producing/production line, producing/production sector.

Produktionsbeschränkung *(f)* — restriction/limitation of production, output restriction.

Produktionsbetrieb *(m)* — producing firm.

Produktionseinrichtungen *(f, Pl)* — production facilities/equipment *(Sg)*.

Produktionseinstellung *(f)* — stoppage/ standstill of production.

Produktionsgang *(m)* — process/phase of production, production process.

Produktionskapazität *(f)* — production/ productive capacity.

Produktionskosten *(Pl)* — cost *(Sg)* of production, production costs.

Produktionsleiter *(m)* — production manager.

Produktionsleitung *(f)* — production/ plant management.

Produktionsmenge *(f)* — production output.

Produktionsmittel *(n, Pl)* — means of production, production equipment.

Produktionsrückgang *(m)* — fall/decrease in production, falling off in production/output.

Produktionssenkung *(f)* —restriction/ limitation of production, output restriction.

Produktionssoll *(n)* — production quota/ target.

Produktionsstand *(m)* — level of production/output.

Produktionsstätte *(f)* — manufacturing/ production plant.

Produktionssteigerung *(f)* — increase in/expansion of production; kräftige Produktionssteigerung: hike in production.

Produktionsstraße *(f)* — production line.

Produktionsumfang *(m)*/ **Produktionsvolumen** *(n)* volume of production.

Produktionswirtschaft *(f)* — producing industry/industries ⟨Pl⟩.

Produktionsziel *(n)* — production target.

Produktionsziffer *(f)* — production/output figure, production/output rate.

Produktionszweig *(m)* — branch of production, industry.

produktiv *(adj)* — productive.

Produktivität *(f)* — productivity.

Produktivitätsgrenze *(f)* — productivity limit/ceiling.

Produktivitätssteigerung *(f)* — increase in productivity.

Produktivitätszulage *(f)* — productivity bonus.

Prokura *(f)* — (power of) procuration, proxy.

Prokurist *(m)* — proxy, authorized/signing clerk.

Promotion *(f)* — obtaining/conferring of a doctorate.

promovieren — to take one's (doctor's) degree, to confer a (doctor's) degree (up-) on.

Proteststreik *(m)* — protest strike.

Provision *(f)* — commission; mit einer Provision von x %: on a x per cent commission.

Provisionsbasis *(f)* — commission, commission basis.

Provisionssatz *(m)* — commission rate.

Prozeß *(m)* — ⟨Klage:⟩ action, ⟨Rechtsstreit:⟩ lawsuit, case, ⟨Strafprozeß:⟩ trial; einen Prozeß gewinnen/verlieren: to win/ to lose a case; einen Prozeß führen: to be engaged in a lawsuit (with s. o.); einen Prozeß anstrengen: to institute legal proceedings (against), to bring an action (against s. o.), to sue s. o.

Prozeßakten *(f, Pl)* — case files/records, pleadings: ⟨vorbereitende Schriftsätze⟩.

Prozeßbevollmächtigte(r) *(f⟨m⟩)* — authorized proxy/agent/attorney.

prozeßfähig *(adj)* — capable to sue and be sued.

Prozeßgegenstand *(m)* — subject of an action.

Prozeßgegner *(m)* — opposing party.

Prozeßkosten *(Pl)* — costs of an action/lawsuit.

Prozeßordnung *(f)* — code/rules ⟨*Pl*⟩ of procedure, court rules ⟨*Pl*⟩.

Prozeßrecht *(n)* — law of practice/procedure, procedural/adjective law.

Prozeßsache *(f)* — legal matter, case.

Prozeßvollmacht *(f)* — power of attorney, retainer, (legal) mandate.

Prüfung *(f)* — examination, trial, test ⟨*Erprobung*⟩; Prüfung mit Auszeichnung bestehen: to pass an examination with hono(u)rs; Prüfung nicht bestehen: to fail in an examination, sich einer Prüfung unterziehen: to sit/to go in for an examination.

Prüfungszeugnis *(n)* — certificate, diploma.

Psychologie *(f)* — psychology.

Pünktlichkeit *(f)* — punctuality, promptness.

Q

Qualifikation *(f)* — qualification, capacity, fitness: ⟨*Eignung*⟩.

qualifiziert *(adj)* — qualified, fit, capable.

Qualitätsprämie *(f)* — quality bonus.

Qualitätsarbeit *(f)* — work of high quality.

Qualitätskontrolle *(f)* — quality control.

Quartalsabrechnung *(f)* **/ Quartalsabschluß** *(m)* — quaterly statement (of accounts).

Querulant *(m)* — querulous/litigious person, troublemaker, crab.

R

Rabatt *(m)* — rebate(ment), abatement, reduction, discount ⟨*Skonto*⟩; Rabatt für Betriebsangehörige: employee discount.

Rädelsführer *(m)* — ringleader, agitator.

Rahmenabkommen *(n)* — skeleton agreement.

Rahmenbestimmung *(f)* — basic rule/regulation.

Rahmengesetz *(n)* — framework/skeleton law.

Rahmentarifvertrag *(m)* — skeleton

tariff/wage agreement.

Rahmenvertrag *(m)* — skeleton contract.

Rangordnung *(f)* — ranking, rank order.

Rationalisierung *(f)* — rationalization.

Rauchverbot *(n)* — order to obstain from smoking.

Realeinkommen *(n)* — real income/revenue/earnings ⟨*Pl*⟩.

Reallohn *(m)* — actual wages.

Rechnungsprüfer *(m)* — controller, accountant.

Rechnungswesen *(n)* — accounting.

Rechtsbeschwerde *(f)* — petition for review on law.

Rechtskenntnisse *(f, Pl)* — legal knowledge.

Rechtsprechung *(f)* — jurisdiction.

Registrator *(m)* — registrar, filing clerk ⟨*BE*⟩, file clerk⟨*AE*⟩.

Regreß *(m)* — recourse, regress; Regreß nehmen: to recover, to seek recovery.

Reife *(f)*, ⟨*mittlere*⟩ — intermediate high school certificate.

Reifezeugnis *(n)* — leaving certificate, General Certificate of Education ⟨*BE*⟩.

Reisekosten *(Pl)* — travel expenses.

Reisekostenabrechnung *(f)* — travel-expense report.

Reisekostenvorschuß *(m)* — travel advance.

Reisespesen *(Pl)* — travel(ling) expenses/charges.

Reisespesen — Tagessatz *(m)* — per-diem allowance.

Reisezeit *(f)* — travel time.

Rente *(f)* — (retiring) pension: ⟨*Altersrente*⟩, annuity ⟨*Jahresrente*⟩.

Rentenzahlung *(f)* — annuity payment.

Reserveoffizier *(m)* — reserve officer, officer of the reserve.

Revisor *(m)* — auditor.

Routinearbeit *(m)* — routine work.

Rückerstattung *(f)* — refund(ment), repayment, reimbursement.

Rückzahlungsvereinbarung *(f)* — repayment agreement/clause.

Ruhegehalt *(n)* — retirement pension, retired pay/pension, (old-age) pension.

Ruhegehaltsempfänger *(m)* — (old-age) pensioner.

Ruhegeldverpflichtung *(f)* — pension liability.

Ruhen *(n)* des Arbeitsverhältnisses — suspension of the employment relationship.

Ruhepause *(f)* — rest (period), recreation time, break.

Ruhestand *(m)* — retirement; im Ruhestand leben: to live in retirement; in den Ruhestand treten: to retire from service, vorzeitiger Ruhestand: early retirement.

Rundschreiben *(n)* — circular (letter).

S

Sachbearbeiter(in) *(m⟨f⟩)* — official in charge.

Sachbezüge *(m, Pl)* — receipts/payment in kind.

Saisonarbeiter(in) *(m⟨f⟩)* — seasonal worker.

Sanitätsraum *(m)* — sick room.

Satzung *(f)* — by-law, statute.

Schadenersatz *(m)* — (payment/ recovery of) damages ⟨*Pl*⟩, damages claim, indemnity, indemnification, compensation, amends ⟨*Pl*⟩; Schadenersatz fordern: to claim/to demand damages; auf Schadenersatz (ver)klagen: to sue (s. o.) for damages; Schadenersatz leisten: to pay/to make payment for damages.

Schadenersatzanspruch *(m)* / **Schadenersatzforderung** *(f)* — claim for damages.

Schadenersatzklage *(f)* — action/suit for damages.

Schadensabteilung *(f)* — claims department/office.

Scheitern *(n)* — failure, breakdown.

Schicht *(f)* — shift, work period ⟨*Arbeitszeit*⟩, bracket ⟨*Gruppe von Arbeitern*⟩.

Schichtarbeit *(f)* — shift work; Schichtarbeit verrichten: to work in shifts.

Schichtarbeiter(in) *(m⟨f⟩)* — shift worker.

Schichtleistung *(f)* — output per (man-) shift.

Schichtlohn *(m)* — pay per shift / for shift work, shift pay.

Schichtmeister *(m)* — overseer.

Schichtplan *(m)* — shift schedule/pattern.

Schichtwechsel *(m)* — shift rotation/changeover, change of shift ⟨*System, nach dem die Schichten planmäßig gewechselt werden*⟩.

Schichtzulage *(f)* — shift premium/allowance.

Schiedsabkommen *(n)* — arbitration agreement.

Schiedsspruch *(m)* — arbitral award.

Schiedsstelle *(f)* — arbitration board.

Schiedsverfahren *(n)* — arbitration proceedings.

schikanieren — to victimise.

Schlechtleistung *(f)* — poor performance.

Schlechtwettergeld *(n)* — bad-weather allowance.

Schlichter(in) *(m⟨f⟩)* — mediator, troubleshooter, arbitrator ⟨*durch Schiedsspruch*⟩, conciliator.

Schlichtung *(f)* — arbitration ⟨*durch Schiedsspruch*⟩, conciliation, mediation.

Schlichtungsausschuß *(m)* — mediation committee.

Schlichtungsvereinbarung *(f)* — amicable agreement (for settling disputes).

Schlichtungsverfahren *(n)* — mediation proceedings ⟨*Pl*⟩, dispute machinery.

Schlichtungsversuch *(m)* — attempt at conciliation/mediation.

Schließung *(f)* ⟨*eines Betriebes*⟩ — closure.

Schlosser *(m)* — locksmith, fitter.

Schlüsselposition *(f)* — key position.

Schmerzensgeld *(n)* — sum of money for injuries suffered, solatium.

Schmiergeld *(n)* — bribe.

Schulabgang *(m)* — leaving school, school-leaving.

Schulungskurs *(m)* — training course, training session.

Schutzanzug *(m)* — protective suit.

Schutzbrille *(f)* — (safety) goggles *(Pl)*.

Schutzgeländer *(n)* — guard rail.

Schutzgitter *(n)* — safety guard, protection fence, protective grid/shutter.

Schutzhandschuh *(m)* — protective glove.

Schutzhaube *(f)* — protective hood.

Schutzhelm *(m)* — safety helmet, hard hat ⟨*bes. bei Bauarbeitern*⟩.

Schutzhülle *(f)* — protective covering/sheathing.

Schutzklausel *(f)* — protective clause.

Schutzkleidung *(f)* — protective clothing.

Schutzmantel *(m)* — protective jacket/case/covering.

Schutzmaske *(f)* — protecting mask, face guard.

Schutzmaßnahmen *(f, Pl)* — protective/ safety measures, precaution(ary) measures.

Schutzschild *(m)* — face shield ⟨*bes. bei Schweißarbeiten*⟩.

Schwangerschaft *(f)* — pregnancy.

Schwarzarbeit *(f)* — illicit/scab work.

Schwerarbeit *(f)* — hard/heavy work.

Schweigepflicht *(f)* — professional secrecy/discretion.

Schwerbehindete(r) *(m⟨f⟩)* — severely handicapped person.

Schwerbehindertengesetz *(n)* — Severely Handicapped Persons Act: ⟨= *Act respecting the employment of severely handicapped persons*⟩.

Schwerpunktstreik *(m)* — selective strike.

Seebetriebsrat *(m)* — fleet works council.

Sekretär(in) *(m⟨f⟩)* ⟨*von jmd*⟩ — secretary ⟨*to s. o.*⟩.

Selbsteinschätzung *(f)* — self-rating, self-appraisal.

Senat *(m)* ⟨*eines Gerichts*⟩ — bench of the Court; Großer Senat — ⟨*beim Bundesarbeitsgericht*⟩ — Great Bench.

Sicherheitsbeauftragter *(m)* — safety official.

Sicherheitsbestimmungen *(f, Pl)* — safety regulations.

Sicherheitseinrichtung *(f)* — safety facility.

Sicherheitsfachkraft *(f)* — (occupational) safety specialist.

Sicherheitsingenieur *(m)* — safety engineer.

Solidaritätsstreik *(m)* — solidarity strike.

Sollarbeitsstunden *(f, Pl)* — nominal manhours.

Solleistung *(f)* — standard output.

Sonderbestimmung *(f)* — special rule, special provision/stipulation/condition/ clause ⟨*jur*⟩.

Sondergenehmigung *(f)* — special permission/authorization, special licence/ -se ⟨*AE*⟩, ⟨*schriftliche:*⟩ special permit.

Sonderleistungen *(f, Pl)* — special services/contributions, soziale Sonderleistungen: fringe benefits.

Sondersitzung *(f)* — special session.

Sondertarif *(m)* — special/preferential tariff.

Sonderurlaub *(m)* — special/extra leave, ⟨*bei Trauerfällen etc.:*⟩ compassionate leave.

Sondervereinbarung *(f)* — special/seperate agreement.

Sondervergütung *(f)* — special/extra allowance, bonus.

Sonderzulage *(f)* — merit increase ⟨*Leistungszulage*⟩, special bonus.

Sonntagsarbeit *(f)* — Sunday working.

Sozialabteilung *(f)* — employee benefit department.

Sozialaufwendungen *(f, Pl)* — social expenditure *(Sg)*.

Sozialbilanz *(f)* — social economic balance sheet.

Sozialeinrichtung *(f)* — social services *(Pl)*.

Sozialeinrichtungen *(f, Pl)* (fig.) — welfare services/facilities.

Sozialgemeinkosten *(Pl)* — fringe benefits.

Sozialhilfe *(f)* — social welfare, public assistance ⟨*AE*⟩, national assistance ⟨*BE*⟩.

Sozialleistungen *(f, Pl)* — social expenditure *(Sg)*, fringe benefits.

Sozialplan *(m)* — social (compensation) plan.

Sozialversicherung *(f)* — social insurance, National Insurance ⟨*BE*⟩, Social Security ⟨*AE*⟩; Leistungen aus der Sozialversicherung: social insurance benefits; staatliche Sozialversicherung: state social security.

Sozialversicherungsbeitrag *(m)* — social insurance contribution, National Insurance contribution ⟨*BE*⟩, Social Security contribution ⟨*AE*⟩.

Sozialversicherungsfreiheit *(f)* — exemption from social insurance.

Sozialversicherungsgrenze *(f)* — (income) limit for social insurance.

Sozialversicherungspflicht *(f)* — obligation to pay social insurance contributions.

Soziologie *(f)* — sociology.

Sparförderung *(f)* ⟨*betriebliche*⟩ — company saving plan/system.

Sparprämie *(f)* — savings premium.

Sparprogramm *(n)* — cost-cutting drive, austerity program(me).

Sperrfrist *(f)* — period of closure, blocking period.

Spesen *(Pl)* — (incidental) expenses, charges, costs ⟨*Kosten*⟩, outlays ⟨*Auslagen*⟩; Spesen abrechnen: to account for expenses; Spesen absetzen: to deduct expenses; die Spesen werden Ihnen erstattet: all expenses will be refunded.

Spesenrichtlinien *(f, Pl)* — expense-account rules.

Spitzenbelastung *(f)* — peak load.

Spitzenleistung *(f)* — peak performance, top efficiency ⟨*Höchstleistung*⟩.

Spitzenlohn *(m)* — maximum wage.

Spitzenposition *(f)* — top spot/position.

Spitzenverdiener *(m)* — top earner.

Sprache *(f)* — language; Beherrschung der Sprache: fluency in language.

Sprachkenntnisse *(f, Pl)* — speaking knowledge.

sprechbehindert — speech-impaired.

Sprecherausschuß *(m)* der leitenden Angestellten — spokesmen committee of the management employees.

Sprechstunde *(f)* — consultation hour, office hours *(Pl)*.

Springer *(m)* — relief man.

Staatsdienst *(m)* — government service, civil service ⟨*BE*⟩, public service ⟨*AE*⟩.

Stabsabteilung *(f)* — staff department.

staffeln ⟨*Arbeitszeit*⟩ — to stagger.

Stammpersonal *(n)* — permanent staff.

Stechuhr *(f)* — time-clock, telltale.

Steigerungsbetrag *(m)* — rate of advance.

Stelle *(f)* — post, position, place, situation, job; eine Stelle suchen: to look for a post; häufig die Stelle wechseln: to job-hop; freie, unbesetzte Stelle: vacant/unoccupied position, vacancy; offene Stelle: job vacancy, unfilled job, open position.

Stellenangebot *(n)* — unfilled job offering, job opportunity/opening, positions offered, ⟨*in Anzeigen:*⟩ personnel wanted.

Stellenanzeige *(f)* — advertisement for a position/post/situation.

Stellenbeschreibung *(f)* — job/position description.

Stellenbesetzungsplan *(m)* — manning table, employee roster.

Stellenbewerber(in) *(m⟨f⟩)* — applicant for a position/post.

Stellenbewerbung *(f)* — application for a position/post.

Stellengesuch *(n)* — application for a post/position, positions wanted.

Stelleninhaber *(m)* — incumbent, job-holder.

Stellenplan *(m)* — staff plan(n)ing/appointment scheme.

Stellensuche *(f)* — job search.

Stellenvermittlung *(f)* — employment/placement agency.

Stellung *(f)* — place, post, position, employment, situation, job; Stellung antreten: to take up a job/position; Stellung aufgeben: to resign from/to throw up one's post; leitende Stellung: executive/leading/managerial position; Stellung suchen: to seek employment, to look for a job; Stellung beibehalten: to stay on the job; in ungekündigter Stellung: not under notice; berufliche Stellung: business standing; feste Stellung: permanent position/job; undkündbare Stellung: permanent tenure.

Stellvertreter *(m)* — substitute, (acting) representative, *⟨amtlicher:⟩* deputy, proxy *⟨Bevollmächtiger⟩*; als Stellvertreter für jmd. fungieren: to act as s. o's deputy, to deputize for s. o.

stempeln *⟨Kontrolluhr⟩* — to clock in/out.

Stempeluhr *(f)* — time clock.

Stenogramm *(n)* — shorthand note.

Stenokontoristin *(f)* — shorthand clerk.

Stenotypistin *(f)* — lady typist.

Sterbegeld *(n)* — death benefit, bereavement pay.

Stichwahl *(f)* — casting vote, additional ballot.

Stillegung *(f)* *⟨eines Werkes⟩* — closure.

stillschweigend *(adj)* — silent, tacit.

Stimmrecht *(n)* — voting right.

Stimmzettel *(m)* — ballot paper, voting paper *⟨AE⟩*; Abstimmung durch Stimmzettel: (voting by) ballot; einen Stimmzettel abgeben: to cast the ballot.

Stipendium *(n)* — scholarship, grant postgraduate scholarship *⟨Forschungsstipendium⟩*, Universitätsstipendium gewähren: to provide university grant.

Strafversetzung *(f)* — disciplinary transfer.

Streik *(m)* — strike, walkout, work stoppage; (un)befristeter Streik: (un)limited strike; wilder Streik: wildcat strike, unofficial strike; illegaler Streik: illegal strike; vom Streik betroffen: struck, strikebound; Streik abbrechen/abblasen *⟨colloq⟩*/beilegen: to call off a strike; Streik ausrufen, zum Streik aufrufen: to call a strike; den Streik fortsetzen: to stay on strike.

Streikabstimmung *(f)* — strike ballot/vote.

streikanfällig *(adj)* — strike-prone.

Streikarbeit *(f)* — work done by non-strikers, strikebreaker's work, black-leg work.

Streikaufruf *(m)* — strike call, call to strike.

Streikausschuß *(m)* — strike committee.

Streikbefehl *(m)* *⟨der Gewerkschaft⟩* — strike order.

Streikbewegung *(f)* — strike movement.

Streikbrecher *(m)* — strikebreaker, blackleg, scab *⟨colloq⟩*.

Streikdrohung *(f)* — strike threat.

streiken *(für)* — to be (out) on strike *(over)* *⟨sich im Streik befinden⟩*, to strike: *⟨in Streik treten⟩*, to go/to come out on strike; to walk out, to refuse (to do it), to cry off, to ba(u)lk, to job: *⟨colloq⟩*.

Streikende(r) *(f⟨m⟩)* — striker.

Streikfonds *(m)* — strike fund.

Streikfront *(f)* — strike/industrial ⟨BE⟩ front.

Streikführer(in) *(m⟨f⟩)* — strike leader.

Streikgefahr *(f)* — danger of a strike.

Streikgegner *(m)* — opponent of a strike.

Streikgeld *(n)* — strike pay.

Streikkasse *(f)* — strike fund.

Streikleitung *(f)* — strike committee.

Streikparole *(f)* — strike slogan.

Streikposten *(m)* — picket; Streikposten stehen: to picket; mit Streikposten besetzen: to picket; mobile Streikposten: flying pickets.

Streikpostenkette *(f)* — picket line.

Streikrecht *(n)* — freedom/right to strike.

Streikunterstützung *(f)* — strike benefit.

Streikverbot *(n)* — prohibition of strike(s), ban on strikes; ein Streikverbot verhängen: to ban, to put a ban on strikes.

Streikwelle *(f)* — wave/series of strikes.

Stückakkord *(m)* — job work.

Stückkosten *(Pl)* — unit cost *(Sg)*.

Stücklohn *(m)* — task wages *(Pl)*, piece wage.

Studienbeihilfe *(f)* — student aid, grant.

Studienrichtung *(f)* — study side.

Studium *(n)* — studies *(Pl)*, study; sein Studium abschließen: to pursue one's studies to the end.

Stundenlohn *(m)* — hourly wage (rate), wage per hour.

Sympathiestreik *(m)* — sympathetic strike.

T

Tagegeld *(n)* — per diem allowance.

Taktzeit *(f)* — work cycle, cycle time.

Tantieme *(f)* — bonus, gratuity.

tantiemeberechtigt *(adj)* **sein** — to be entitled to a bonus.

Tarif *(m)* — wage/salary scale, scale (of wages/salaries); gleitender Tarif: sliding scale; über/unter Tarif bezahlt werden: to be paid above/below agreed wage/salary scale.

Tarifabkommen *(n)* — trade/bargaining agreement.

Tarifabschluß *(m)* — tariff settlement.

Tarifänderung *(f)* — change of/in tariff.

Tarifangestellte(r) *(m⟨f⟩)* — employee covered by/under collective agreement, scale-wage employee.

Tarifausschuß *(m)* — tariff committee, wages council/board/committee.

Tarifautonomie *(f)* — autonomy in negotiating wage rates: ⟨Lohnverhandlungen⟩.

Tarifbestimmungen *(f, Pl)* — tariff regulations, wage regulations.

Tarifbezirk *(m)* — collective-agreement area.

Tariferhöhung *(f)* — increase in scale wages/salaries, increase of standard wage.

Tariffähigkeit *(f)* — bargaining power.

Tariffestsetzung *(f)* — fixing of the tariff.

Tarifforderung *(f)* — tariff claim.

Tariffront *(f)* — wage/wages ⟨BE⟩ front.

Tarifgebiet *(n)* — tariff area/region.

Tarifgehalt *(n)* – collective agreed/scale salary.

Tarifgestaltung *(f)* – collective wage formation.

Tarifgruppe *(f)* – tariff wage group.

Tarifhoheit *(f)* – right to conclude collective agreements.

tarifieren – to tariff.

Tarifklasse *(f)* – tariff class, wage-rate bracket.

Tarifkommission *(f)* – tariff commission, commission for collective wage agreement: ⟨*Lohnverhandlungen*⟩, collective bargaining commission.

Tarifkonflikt *(m)* – wage/salaries dispute.

Tarifkündigung *(f)* – (notice of) termination of scale of rates/charges, (notice of) termination of agreed wages/salaries.

tariflich *(adj)* – according to tariff, according to wage scale (agreed), as per tariff, tariff-wise.

Tariflohn *(m)* – contractual/agreed/ standard wage(s), union rate.

Tarifordnung *(f)* – wage scale/schedule, pay scale/wages regulations ⟨*Pl*⟩.

Tarifpartner *(m)* – party to a (collective) wage agreement; die Tarifpartner ⟨*Pl*⟩: the employers and the employed.

Tarifpolitik *(f)* – wage(-scale) policy: ⟨*bei Lohnverhandlungen*⟩.

Tarifrunde *(f)* – collective bargaining/ wages round.

Tarifsatz *(m)* – agreed wage/standard rate.

Tarifstruktur *(f)* – tariff/wage rate structure.

Tarifsystem *(n)* – tariff(ing) system.

Tariftabelle *(f)* – tariff, scale of rates.

Tarifurlaub *(m)* – collectively agreed holidays *(Pl)*/vacation ⟨*AE*⟩.

Tarifvereinbarung *(f)* – collective bargaining agreement.

Tarifverhandlungen *(f, Pl)* – collective bargaining, tariff negotiations *(Pl)*.

Tarifvertrag *(m)* – ⟨*Entgelttarifvertrag:*⟩ wage/tariff agreement, ⟨*Manteltarifvertrag:*⟩ employment conditions agreement, ⟨*Lohn-/Gehaltsrahmentarifvertrag:*⟩ wage/salary structure agreement, collective (bargaining) agreement; Tarifvertrag aushandeln: to negotiate an industrial agreement, to bargain collectively.

Tarifvertragsgesetz *(n)* – Collective Agreements Act.

Tätigkeit *(f)* – activity, work ⟨*Arbeit*⟩, occupation, employment ⟨*Beschäftigung*⟩; berufliche Tätigkeit: professional employment; ehrenamtliche Tätigkeit: honorary service/position; gewerkschaftliche Tätigkeit: union activity; selbständige Tätigkeit: self-employment; unselbständige Tätigkeit: payroll employment.

Tätigkeitsbereich *(m)* – field of activity.

Tätigkeitsbeschreibung *(f)* – job description.

Teilversammlung *(f)* – sectional meeting.

Teilzahlung *(f)* – part(ial) payment, initial payment, payment in part/on account, instalment (payment).

Teilzeitarbeit *(f)* – part-time work.

Tendenzbetrieb *(m)* – ideological establishment.

Teuerungszuschlag *(m)* – cost of living allowance ('COLA').

Torkontrolle *(f)* – exit/gate control, security control.

Trennungszulage *(f)* – separation allowance.

Treu *(f)* **und Glaube** *(m)* ⟨*Ausdr.*⟩ — good faith.

Treuepflicht *(f)* ⟨*des Arbeitnehmers*⟩ — obligation for loyalty/faith.

U

überarbeiten, sich — to overstrain o. s.

Überbelastung *(f)* — overload.

Überbrückungsbeihilfe *(f)* — stopgap/interim aid, bridge payment.

Überstunde *(f)* — overtime work, overtime/extra hour.

Überstundenbezahlung *(f)* — overtime pay.

Überstundenverbot *(n)* — overtime ban.

Überstundenzuschlag *(m)* — overtime premium/bonus.

Überwachungseinrichtung *(f)* — monitoring device/equipment.

Übung *(f)* ⟨*betriebliche*⟩ — established operating practices *(Pl)*.

umbestellen — to redirect.

Umdeutung *(f)* ⟨*einer Kündigung*⟩ — reinterpretation (of a termination).

Umgruppierung *(f)* — re-classification, regrading.

Umkleideraum *(m)* — changing room.

Umsatzbeteiligung *(f)* — participation in sales/in the turnover.

Umschulung *(f)* — retraining, re-education.

umsetzen ⟨*Arbeitskräfte*⟩ — to dislocate, to transfer.

Umweltschutz *(m)* — environmental protection.

Umweltschutzbeauftragte(r) *(f⟨m⟩)* — environment protection representative.

umziehen — to relocate, to remove.

Umzug *(m)* — relocation, move ⟨*AE*⟩, remove ⟨*BE*⟩.

Umzugskosten *(Pl)* — removal expenses.

Umzugskostenbeihilfe *(f)* — removal allowance ⟨*BE*⟩, transfer allowance ⟨*AE*⟩.

Unabdingbarkeit *(f)* ⟨*jur*⟩ — inalienability.

Unabkömmlichstellung *(f)* ⟨*vom Wehrdienst*⟩ — deferment.

unbegabt *(adj)* — untalented, ungifted.

unbescholten *(adj)* — spotless.

unbezahlt *(adj)* — unpaid, without pay; unbezahlter Urlaub: leave without pay.

unentschuldigt *(adj)* —; unentschuldigtes Fehlen: absence without leave.

unfähig *(adj)* — incapable, unfit.

Unfall *(m)* — accident; meldepflichtiger Unfall: reportable accident.

Unfallbericht *(m)* — injury investigation report.

Unfallhäufigkeitsrate *(f)* ⟨= *Unfälle je 1 Mio Arbeitsstunden*⟩ — accident frequency rate.

Unfallschwereart *(f)* ⟨= *Ausfalltage je 1 Mio Arbeitsstunden*⟩ — accidentsevertiy rate.

Unfallschutz *(m)* — accident prevention.

Unfallursachen *(f, Pl)* — causes of accident.

Unfallverhütung *(f)* — accident prevention.

Unfallverhütungsvorschriften *(f, Pl)* — safety regulations.

Unfallversicherung *(f)* — accident insurance.

Unfallversicherungs-(Neuregelungs-) Gesetz *(n)* — Accident Insurance (Reorganizing) Act ⟨= *Act to reorganize the law governing the statutory accident insurance scheme*⟩.

ungekündigt *(adj)* — not under notice.

ungelernt *(adj)* — unskilled, untrained ⟨*unausgebildet*⟩.

Universitätsstudium *(n)* — academic training, university education.

Universitätsexamen *(n)* — university degree.

unkündbar *(adj)* — irrevocable, binding.

Unmöglichkeit *(f)* ⟨*der Arbeitsleistung*⟩ — impossibility of work/performance.

unselbständig *(adj)* — dependent, unselbstständige Arbeit *(f)*: employment work.

Untergebene(r) *(f ⟨m⟩)* — subordinate.

Unterhalt *(m)* — maintenance, support, ⟨*an geschiedene Ehefrau:*⟩ alimony.

unterhaltsberechtigt *(adj)* — ⟨*Ehefrau:*⟩ entitled to alimony, ⟨*Kind:*⟩ entitled to maintenance.

Unternehmen *(n)* — enterprise, undertaking.

Unternehmensberater *(m)* — management counsel(l)or/consultant.

Unternehmensverfassung *(f)* — constitution of an enterprise.

Unterrichtungspflicht *(f)* — obligation to inform.

Unterschriftsvollmacht *(f)* — authority to sign, signing power.

Unterschriftensammlung *(f)* — collection of signatures, sign-in.

unterstellt sein — to be subordinated to s. o.

Unterstützung *(f)* — support, relief ⟨*Fürsorge*⟩, assistance, aid ⟨*Hilfe*⟩.

Unterstützungskasse *(f)* — support fund.

Untersuchung *(f)* ⟨*ärztliche*⟩ — medical examination.

Unvermögen *(n)* — inability.

unzuverlässig *(adj)* — unreliable, incalculable.

Urabstimmung *(f)* — initial vote, strike ballot.

Urlaub *(m)* — holiday, vacation ⟨*AE*⟩, leave.

Urlaubsabgeltung *(f)* — compensation for holidays/vacation ⟨*AE*⟩ not taken.

Urlaubsanspruch *(m)* — vacation entitlement.

Urlaubsentgelt *(n)* — payment during leave, vacation compensation (pay) ⟨*AE*⟩, vacation payment.

Urlaubsgeld *(n)* ⟨*zusätzliches*⟩ — vacation bonus/benefit.

Urlaubsgrundsätze *(m, Pl)* — principles for leave arrangements.

Urlaubsplan *(m)* — leave/vacation ⟨*AE*⟩ schedule.

Urlaubsvertretung *(f)* — holiday ⟨*BE*⟩/vacation ⟨*AE*⟩ replacement.

Urwahl *(f)* — primary election.

V

verantwortlich *(adj)* — responsible.

Verantwortung *(f)* — responsibility.

Verantwortungsbereich *(m)* — area of responsibility.

Verbesserungsvorschlag *(m)* — suggestion, proposal.

Verdienst *(m, n)* — earnings *(Pl)*, income, merit; jmd. nach seinen Verdiensten *(n, Pl)* einschätzen: to rate s. o. according to his merits/deserts; dies ist das Verdienst von X: the credit for this goes to X; seine Verdienste um: his services to.

Verdienstausfall *(m)* — loss of remuneration/earnings *(Pl)*.

Verdienstbescheinigung *(f)* — statement of earnings.

Verdienstmöglichkeit *(f)* — earning possibility.

vereinbaren — to agree, to settle, to stipulate; Gehalt vereinbaren: to appoint a salary; stillschweigend vereinbaren: to stipulate tacitly; vertraglich vereinbaren: to stipulate by contract.

Vereinbarung *(f)* — agreement, settlement, stipulation; ausdrückliche Vereinbarung: express agreement; gütliche Vereinbarung: amicable settlement; mündliche Vereinbarung: verbal/oral agreement; Vereinbarung abschließen: to conclude an agreement.

Verfahren *(n)* — operation ⟨*Arbeitsvorgang*⟩, process, technique ⟨*Herstellung*⟩, manner, method ⟨*Methode*⟩, procedure.

Verfallfrist *(f)* — expiring date.

Verfügung *(f)* — disposition, provision, direction ⟨*Anordnung*⟩, decree, order ⟨*Verordnung*⟩, einstweilige Verfügung: interim injunction, restraining, provisional order.

Vergabe *(f)* von Arbeiten *(Pl)* nach außerhalb ⟨*Ausdr.*⟩ — contracting out.

Vergleich *(m)* — compromise, settlement, arrangement, ⟨*mit Gläubigern:*⟩ composition; durch Vergleich abfinden: to compound with; Abfindung durch Vergleich: composition; gütlicher Vergleich: amicable settlement.

Vergütung *(f)* — remuneration, pay(ment), reward, gratuity ⟨*Belohnung*⟩, compensation ⟨*Entschädigung*⟩, fee ⟨*Honorar*⟩, emoluments, perquisites ⟨*BE*⟩: ⟨*besondere Bezüge*⟩.

Verhaltenwissenschaft *(f)* — behavioural science.

Verhandlung *(f)* — negotiation (on, about, over, for), bargaining (on, about), talk (on, about); Verhandlung abbrechen: to break off negotiations; Verhandlung aufnehmen/in Verhandlung eintreten: to take up/to enter into/to open/to start/to initiate negotiations; Verhandlungen *(Pl)* führen: to conduct negotiations.

Verhandlungsergebnis *(n)* — negotiation outcome; vorläufiges Verhandlungsergebnis: provisional agreement.

Verhandlungsgegenstand *(m)* — object of/matter for negotiation; Verhandlungsgegenstand sein: to be under negotiation.

verhaltensbedingt *(adj)* — conduct related.

verjähren — to come under / to be barred by the statute of limitation(s).

Verjährung *(f)* — limitation (of time), statute of limitation(s), ⟨*eines Besitzrechtes:*⟩ prescription.

Verjährungsfrist *(f)* — period/term of limitation.

Vermittlungsausschuß *(m)* — mediation/conciliation committee.

Vermittlungsverfahren *(n)* — conciliation proceedings *(Pl)*.

Vermögensbildung *(f)* — capital accumulation.

Vermögensbildungsgesetz *(n)* — Capital Accumulation Act: ⟨= *Act to encourage the accumulation of capital by employees*⟩.

Vermögenswirksame Anlage *(f)* — capital-forming investment under the employees' saving scheme.

Vermögenswirksame Leistung *(f)* — (employer's) capital-forming payment under the employees' saving scheme.

Versager *(m)* — breakdown, flop, washout; Versager sein: to flunk.

Verschulden *(n)* — negligence.

verschweigen *⟨arglistig⟩* — to conceal *⟨fraudently⟩*.

Verschwiegenheit *(f)* — discretion, secrecy.

Verschwiegenheitspflicht *(f)* — obligation to discretion.

versetzen —to transfer, to move.

Versetzung *(f)*— transfer, shift(ing), removal, displacement, *⟨örtlich:⟩* relocation.

Versicherungspflicht *(f)* — liability to insure, obligation to insure, compulsory insurance.

Versicherungspflichtgrenze *(f)*— insurance liability limit.

Versorgung *(f)* *⟨ärztliche⟩* — medical care.

Versorgungsanwartschaft *(f)*— eligibility for a pension.

Versorgungszusage *(f)* — pension pledge.

Verteilzeit *(f)* *⟨persönliche⟩* — relief time.

Verteilzeitaufnahme *(f)* — log.

Vertrag *(m)*— contract, agreement; Vertrag (ab)schließen: to make, to conclude a contract; aufgrund eines Vertrages: under an agreement; Anspruch aus einem Vertrag: claim under a contract; Vertrag aufheben: to cancel/to rescind an agreement.

vertraglich *(adj)* — contractual.

vertragsbrüchig *(adj)*— contract-breaking.

Vertragsfreiheit *(f)* — freedom of contract.

Vertragsstrafe *(f)*— contractual penalty.

Vertragsverhältnis *(n)*— contractual relation(ship).

Vertrauensarzt *(m)* — health officer, medical examiner.

Vertrauensmann *(m)* **/ Vertrauensperson** *(f)* *⟨im Betrieb⟩* — shop steward.

Vertrauensmann *(m)* **der Schwerbehinderten** — disabled persons' representative.

Vertrauensstellung *(f)* — confidential post, position of trust.

vertraulich *(adj)* — confidential.

Vertretung *(f)* — *⟨im Amt:⟩* substitution, replacement *⟨Ersatz⟩*.

Verwaltung *(f)* — administration.

Verwaltungsgericht *(n)*— administrative court.

Verwaltungspersonal *(n)* — administrative personnel/staff.

Verwarnung *(f)* — warning, reprimand.

Verweis *(m)* — reproof, reprimand, censure; Verweis erteilen (wegen): to reprimand/to rebuke/to censure s. o. for, give s. o. a rap on/over the knuckles: *⟨colloq⟩*.

Verwirkung *(f)*— forfeiture.

Verzicht *(m)* *⟨jur⟩*— renunciation, waiver.

Vielseitigkeitstraining *(n)* — versatility training.

Volksschulbildung *(f)* — elementary/primary education.

Vollbeschäftigung *(f)* — full employment.

volljährig *(adj)*— major, of age; volljährig sein: to be of (full) age.

Vollmacht *(f)* —power, full powers, authority; Vollmacht erteilen: to empower, to authorize.

Volontär *(m)* — volunteer, trainee⟨*AE*⟩.

Vorarbeiter *(m)* — foreman, master mechanic.

Vorauswahl *(f)* —pre-selection.

vorbestraft *(adj)*— previously convicted.

Vorbildung *(f)* — educational background ⟨*Erziehung*⟩, required qualification ⟨*Ausbildung*⟩.

Vorgabeleistung *(f)* — standard (performance).

Vorgabezeiten *(f, Pl)* — time standards.

Vorgabezeitermittlung *(f)*— rate setting.

Vorgesetzter *(m)* — superior, supervisory employee; unmittelbarer Vorgesetzter: immediate superior.

Vorhol-/Nachholtag *(m)* — make-up-day.

Vormundschaft *(f)* — guardianship; unter Vormundschaft stehen: to be under guardianship.

Vorruhestand *(m)* — pre-retirement.

Vorschlagswesen *(n)* ⟨*(inner-)betriebliches*⟩ — employee suggestion scheme; Prämie im Vorschlagswesen: suggestion (program) award.

Vorschuß(zahlung) *(f)* — (payment) in advance, advance payment, anticipation, payment on account.

Vorsorgeuntersuchung *(f)* — medical checkup.

Vorstand *(m)* — executive/management board.

Vorstellung *(f)* — employment interview: ⟨*bei Bewerbung*⟩; persönliche Vorstellung erwünscht: personal attendance required.

Vorstellungsgespräch *(n)* — (personal) interview.

Vorstrafe *(f)* — previous conviction.

Vorstrafenregister *(n)* — police/criminal report.

W

Wahl *(f)* — election, choice, selection: ⟨*Auswahl*⟩, election, ballot; Wahl anfechten: to contest an election; geheime Wahl: secret vote.

Wahlanfechtung *(f)* — election contest, contesting of an election.

Wahlausschreiben *(n)* — declaration of the elections.

wählbar *(adj)* — eligible.

wahlberechtigt *(adj)* — having voting rights, entitled to vote.

Wahlbewerber *(m)* — candidate, applicant.

Wählerliste *(f)* — voters' list.

Wahlmann *(m)* — delegate, elector ⟨*AE*⟩.

Wahlvorstand *(m)* — electoral board.

Wahlzettel *(m)* — ballot/voting paper.

Wanderarbeiter *(m)* — migrant worker.

Wärmebetrieb *(m)* — heat treat operation.

Warnstreik *(m)* — warning strike.

Wartezeit *(f)* — waiting period, qualifying period, attendance time ⟨*Zeitstudie*⟩.

Wartungspersonal *(n)* — maintenance personnel.

Wehrdienst *(m)* — military service.

Wehrdienstverweigerer *(m)* — conscientious objector.

wehrpflichtig *(adj)* — liable to military service.

Wehrpflichtiger *(m)* − draftee.

Wehrübung *(f)* − reserve duty training.

Weihnachtsgeld *(n)* − Christmas bonus.

Weihnachtsgratifikation *(f)* − Christmas bonus.

weisungsgebunden *(adj)* − subject to directions.

Weisungsrecht *(n)* − right to give directions/instructions.

Weiterbeschäftigung *(f)* − continued employment.

Werdegang *(m)* − resume.

Werksangehörige(r) *(f⟨m⟩)* − employee.

Werksicherheit *(f)* / **Werkschutz** *(m)* ⟨*zur Sicherung der Anlagen*⟩ − plant security.

Werkskantine *(f)* − canteen, catering department.

Werkstatt *(f)* − workshop.

Werksurlaub *(m)* − plant shut-down.

Werkswohnung *(f)* − company owned/sponsored housing for employees.

Werktag *(m)* − workday; working day.

Werkvertrag *(m)* − contract for work and service.

Werkzeugmacher *(m)* − tool-maker.

Wertpapiersparplan *(m)* − share savings scheme.

Wertminderung *(f)* − depreciation.

Wettbewerbsklausel *(f)* − competitive/restraint clause.

Wettbewerbsverbot *(n)* − restraint of trade.

Widerspruchsstelle *(f)* − appeal committee.

wiederaufnehmen ⟨*Arbeit*⟩ − to resume work.

Wiedereingewöhnung *(f)* − recovery.

Wiedereingliederung *(f)* − ⟨*berufliche:*⟩ ⟨*vocational*⟩ rehabilitation, ⟨*soziale:*⟩ resettlement.

Wiedereinstellung *(f)* − reemployment, rehiring, reappointment, re-instatement.

Wirkungsbereich *(m)* − sphere of action, scope of activities.

Wirtschaftsausschuß *(m)* − economic committee.

Wirtschaftshilfe *(f)* − economic aid.

Wirtschaftslage *(f)* − economic situation/activity.

Wochenarbeitszeit *(f)* − hours worked per week.

Wochenlohn *(m)* − weekly pay.

Wohngeldzuschuß *(m)* − lodging allowance/money, allowance for room/rent.

Wohnsitz *(m)* − residence, place of abode.

Wohnung *(f)* − accomodation, flat, housing.

Wohnungsbaudarlehen *(n)* − housing loan.

Z

zahlungsfähig *(adj)* − solvent.

zeichnungsberechtigt *(adj)* − authorized to sign.

Zeit *(f)* − time; Systeme vorbestimmter Zeiten *(Pl):* predetermined-elemental-time standards.

Zeitarbeit *(f)* − job leasing, temporary employment.

Zeitaufnahmebogen *(m)* — time study sheet.

Zeitkontrolle *(f)* — timekeeping.

Zeitlohn *(m)* — straight time pay, flat rate pay system.

Zeitstudie *(f)* — time study.

Zeitstudieningenieur *(m)* — time-study engineer. ·

Zeugnis *(n)* — report ⟨*Schulzeugnis*⟩, certificate, credential ⟨*Prüfungszeugnis*⟩, reference, testimonial, character ⟨*Führungszeugnis*⟩; seine Zeugnisse *(Pl)* vorlegen: to present one's credentials; jmd. ein Zeugnis ausstellen: to write s. o. a reference, attestation, witness ⟨*Bescheinigung*⟩, ⟨*ärztliches:*⟩ medical certificate, doctor's certificate.

Zeugnisabschrift *(f)* — copy of a certificate/diploma; beglaubigte Zeugnisabschrift: certified/exemplified copy of a diploma.

Zeugnisverweigerungsrecht *(n)* — right to refuse to give evidence.

Zivildienst *(m)* — civilian service.

Zivilprozeßordnung *(f)* — Code of Civil Procedure.

Zugang *(m)* der Kündigung — receipt/arrival of the notice of termination.•

Zurückbehaltung *(f)* ⟨*der Arbeitsleistung*⟩ — retention ⟨*of work*⟩.

Zurückbehaltungsrecht *(n)* — right of retention.

Zurückstellung *(f)* vom Wehrdienst — exemption from service.

Zusatzurlaub *(m)* — supplementary holiday/vacation ⟨*AE*⟩.

Zusatzversicherung *(f)* — supplementary insurance.

Zuschlag *(m)* — extra charge, bonus, premium ⟨*Gratifikation*⟩.

Zuschuß *(m)* — allowance, allocation ⟨*Unterhaltszuschuß*⟩, subsidy, grant ⟨*staatlicher Zuschuß*⟩, pecuniary aid.

zuständig *(adj)* — competent.

Zuständigkeit *(f)* — competency.

zustimmen — to agree, to approve.

zuweisen — to assign, to allocate.

Zwangsarbeiter *(m)* — displaced person.

Zwangsbeitrag *(m)* — compulsory contribution.

Zwangsschlichtung *(f)* — compulsory arbitration.

Zwischenprüfung *(f)* — intermediate examination.

Foreword

In the course of the increasing international economic interdependence and the growing cooperation of companies across borders, a continous interchange of information in the field of personnel matters has developed. The interchange, which will be of increasing importance following the completion of the Single European Market, takes place in different ways:

There are numerous publications on personnel matters. There is also the interchange of ideas and experience in international meetings and conferences as well as direct contacts with personnel from foreign companies.

This pocket-dictionary is meant for professionals working in personnel matters who have to communicate in the German language. It should help the user to find the correct translation for the most common terms and expressions. It consists of terms from the personnel field in the broadest sense and includes everyday legal terms, particularly those relating to labour law. New formations of words are often difficult to understand without being supplement by root-words. Therefore root-words are included where regarded as necessary or helpful.

This dictionary depending on its destination, requires basic knowledge in both languages. When using it, it should be recognized, that the personnel function and consequently the respective terminology are subject to change. New techniques are applied, new functions developed and new stipulations are issued, for which new terms and phrases have to be formed. This is the reason why a dictionary of this kind can never be complete.

The author and the publisher would, therefore, appreciate any kind of suggestion for additions and improvement as well as corrections of any errors found. The publisher gratefully accepts all expert submissions for possible inclusions in subsequent editions.

Cologne, September 1988   Author and Publisher

Advice to the User

— Catchwords are principally compiled in alphabetical order, heavy typed and seperated by a paragraph.

— The classification of a word as catchword or its subgroupings under a catchword is attributable to the grade of its independency.

— The catchword is separated from its translation by horizontal stroke. The translation of a catchword's subgrouping is put behind a colon.

— In case there is more than one translation for a catchword, the translations are separated by a comma.

— A diagonal stroke separates synonyms of a word or an expression. Synonyms placed immediately ahead or behind the diagonal stroke ma be exchanged. The meaning of the word or expression remains unchanged.

— Plural forms have been arranged in the same alphabetical order as the singular. They have been marked by *(Pl)*.

— In the German-English section the english verbs have been marked by a preceding "to", in the English-German section by a following *(v)*. German verbs have not been marked.

— German masculine nouns indicating a person who is acting or doing something mostly form the corresponding feminine by the addition of "-in". In such cases the addition is placed in round brackets.

e. g. Arbeiter(in) *(m ⟨f⟩)*

— In the case of German masculine nouns whose endings vary according to the qualifiying article, the word is given in the form which follows the indefinite article.

e. g. Handlungsreisender *(m)*

signifying "der Handlungsreisende" as well as "ein Handlungsreisender".

- When the same form of a German noun is used for both the feminine and the masculine it is given as

  e. g. Angestellte(r) *(f ⟨m⟩)*

  signifying **der, die** and **eine** Angestellte, as well as **ein** Angestellter.

- Round brackets

  ○ following a noun enclose the indication of the number of the noun *(Pl)*, *(Sg)* and the part of speech *(adj)*, *(adv)*, *(v)*

  ○ enclose words or parts of words which may be read or committed without changing the sense. Thus

    e. g. Förder(ungs)unterricht

    signifies that both "Förderungsunterricht" and "Förderunterricht" may be used with exactly the same meaning.

  ○ within a word enclose single letters or a part of the word which allow an additional form of spelling. e. g. labo(ou)r

- Cornered brackets enclose an explanation or an extension of the catchword.

Erläuterungen der angewandten Abkürzungen
Explanation of abbreviations used

adj.	— Adjektiv	— adjective
adv.	— Adverb.	— adverb
AE	— hauptsächlich in den Vereinigten Staaten gebräuchlich	— chiefly used in the U. S.
Ausdr.	— Ausdruck	— expression
BE	— hauptsächlich in Groß- britannien gebräuchlich	— chiefly used in the U. K.
bes.	— besonders	— especially
colloq.	— Umgangssprache	— colloquial
etc.	— et cetera	— and so on
f	— Feminium/weiblich	— feminine
jmd.	— jemand(en)	— someone
jur.	— juristisch	— legal
m	— Masculinum/männlich	— masculine
med.	— medizinisch	— medical
mil.	— militärisch	— military
n	— Neutrum/sächlich	— neuter
o., one's	— ein, eines	— one, one's
o. s.	— sich (selbst)	— oneself
Pl.	— Plural/Mehrzahl	— plural
Sg.	— Singular/Einzahl	— singular
s. o.	— jemand	— someone
s. th.	— etwas	— something
techn.	— technisch	— technical
v	— Verb	— verb

A

abatement — Rabatt *(m)*, Ermäßigung *(f)*.

ability — Befähigung *(f)*, Fähigkeit *(f)*, Können *(n)*; ability requirement: Fähigkeitsanforderung *(f)*; ability to earn a livelihood: Erwerbsfähigkeit *(f)*; ability to perform: Arbeitsfähigkeit *(f)*.

able *(adj)* — fähig, befähigt, tüchtig; able to make contracts: geschäftsfähig; able to work: arbeitsfähig, tauglich; able-bodied *(adj)*: kräftig, gesund, diensttauglich ⟨*mil*⟩.

absence — Abwesenheit *(f)*; absence from work: Arbeitsversäumnis *(n)*.

absent *(adj)* — abwesend, fehlend.

absenteeism — Fernbleiben von der Arbeit *(n)*, Abwesenheit *(f)*; absenteeism rate: Abwesenheitsrate *(f)*.

academic(-al) *(adj)* — akademisch; academic training: Universitätsstudium *(n)*.

accident — Unfall *(m)*; accident at work: Arbeitsunfall *(m)*; accident benefit: Unfallentschädigung *(f)*; accident insurance: Unfallversicherung *(f)*; Accident Insurance-(Reorganisation)Act ⟨*Act to reorganize the law governing the statutory accident insurance scheme*⟩: Unfallversicherungs-(Neuregelungs-)Gesetz *(n)*; accident prevention: Unfallverhütung *(f)*; accident-frequency-rate: Unfallhäufigkeitsrate *(f)* ⟨*Unfälle je 1 Mio Arbeitsstunden*⟩; accident-severity rate: Unfallschwereart *(f)* ⟨*Ausfalltage je 1 Mio Arbeitsstunden*⟩.

accomodation — Wohnung *(f)*.

account — Konto *(n)*.

accountability — Haftpflicht *(f)*,Verantwortlichkeit *(f)*.

accountant — Rechnungsprüfer(in) *(m ⟨f⟩)*.

accounting — Rechnungswesen *(n)*.

achievement — Arbeitsergebnis *(n)*; achievement motivation: Leistungsmotivation *(f)*.

acquaint o. s. *(v)* — sich einarbeiten.

acting *(adj)* — geschäftsführend; acting in good faith: gutgläubig; acting representative: Stellvertreter(in) *(m ⟨f⟩)*.

action — Tätigkeit *(f)*, Klage *(f)*, Prozeß *(m)*; subject of an action: Prozeßgegenstand *(m)*; action for damages: Schadenersatzklage *(f)*.

active *(adj)* — emsig, geschäftig, energisch; active service: Militärdienst *(m)*.

activity — Tätigkeit *(f)*, Beschäftigung *(f)*, Wirkungskreis *(m)*.

actual wage — Effektivlohn *(m)*; actual wages *(Pl)*: Reallohn *(m)*.

ad ⟨*AE*⟩ — Inserat *(n)*, Annonce *(f)*.

additional *(adj)* — zusätzlich, ergänzend; additional ballot : Stichwahl *(f)*; additional income: Nebeneinkünfte *(Pl)*; additional work: Mehrarbeit *(f)*.

adjective law — Prozeßrecht *(n)*.

administration — Verwaltung *(f)*.

administrative court — Verwaltungsgericht *(n)*.

administrative personnel/staff — Verwaltungspersonal *(n)*.

adult education course — Fortbildungskurs(-us) *(m)*, Fortbildungslehrgang *(m)*.

advance *(v)* — bevorschussen, aufsteigen ⟨*Karriere*⟩; advance on salary: Gehaltsvorschuß *(m)*; advance payment: Vorschuß(-zahlung) *(m/f)*.

advanced training — Fortbildung *(f)*.

advancement — Förderung *(f)*.

adverse *(adj)* **to labo(u)r** — arbeitsscheu.

advertisement — Inserat *(n)*, Annonce *(f)*; advertisement for a position: Stellenanzeige *(f)*.

affidavit — Eid *(m)*.

age — Alter *(n)*; age allowance/exemption: Altersfreibetrag *(m)*; age distribution/structure: Altersstruktur *(f)*, Altersaufbau *(m)*; age limit: Altersgrenze *(f)*.

agitator — Rädelsführer *(m)*.

agree *(v)* — sich einigen, übereinstimmen, zustimmen, vereinbaren; agreed wage: Tariflohn *(m)*; agreed wage/standard rate: Tarifrate *(f)*.

agreement — Vereinbarung *(f)*, Abkommen *(n)*; come *(v)* to an agreement: sich einigen.

aid — Hilfe *(f)*, Gehilfe *(m)*, Gehilfin *(f)*.

alien — Fremder *(m)*, Ausländer *(m)*; alien's residence permit: Aufenthaltserlaubnis *(f)* ⟨*für Ausländer*⟩.

alimony — Unterhalt *(m)* ⟨*an geschiedene Ehefrau*⟩.

allocate *(v)* — zuteilen, zuweisen; allocate duties: Pflichten *(f, Pl)* zuweisen; allocate expenses: Unkosten *(Pl)* verteilen, Gemeinkosten *(Pl)* umlegen.

allot *(v)* — auslosen, verteilen, zuteilen, bewilligen.

allowance — Beihilfe *(f)*, Zuschuß *(m)*, Vergütung *(f)*, Entschädigung *(f)*; allowance for room/rent: Wohngeldzuschuß *(m)*; allowance in kind: Deputat *(n)*.

alteration of an establisment — Betriebsänderung *(f)*.

ambition — Ehrgeiz *(m)*.

amendment — Änderungsvorschlag *(m)* ⟨*zu einem Gesetz*⟩.

amends *(Pl)* — Schadenersatz *(m)*, Wiedergutmachung *(f)*.

amicable *(adj)* — gütlich; amicable agreement: Schlichtungsvereinbarung *(f)*; amicable settlement: gütliches Abkommen *(n)*.

ancillary workers *(Pl)* — Hilfspersonal *(n)*.

anniversary — Jubiläum *(n)*.

annual *(adj)* — jährlich; annual adjustment of income tax: Lohnsteuerjahresausgleich *(m)*; annual general meeting: Jahreshauptversammlung *(f)*; annual holiday/leave: Jahresurlaub *(m)*; annual income: Jahreseinkommen *(n)*; annual rent: Grundrente *(f)*.

annuity — (Jahres-) Rente *(f)*; annuity payment: Rentenzahlung *(f)*.

answerable *(adj)* — haftbar, verantwortlich.

anti-union *(adj)* — gewerkschaftsfeindlich.

anticipation — Vorschußzahlung *(f)*.

apartment ⟨*AE*⟩ — Wohnung *(f)*.

appeal (against) — förmliche Beschwerde *(f)* (gegen) ⟨*jur*⟩, Berufung *(f)* ⟨*jur*⟩; appeal procedure: Beschwerdeverfahren *(n)* ⟨*Verfahrensweise*⟩; appeal proceedings: Beschwerdeverfahren *(n)* ⟨*Verhandlungen*⟩.

appelate court — Berufungsgericht *(n)*, Oberlandesgericht *(n)*.

applicant for a post/position — Stellenbewerber(in) *(m* ⟨*f*⟩*)*.

application — Bewerbung *(f)*; application blank ⟨*AE*⟩: Bewerbungsformular *(n)*, Bewerbungsbogen *(m)*; application for a post/position: Stellengesuch *(n)*, Stellenbewerbung *(f)*; application papers *(Pl)*: Bewerbungsunterlagen *(f, Pl)*.

apply for *(v)* — sich bewerben um/für.

appoint *(v)* — ernennen.

appointment — Ernennung *(f)*, Anstellung *(f)*.

appraisal — Beurteilung *(f)*.

apprentice — Lehrling *(m)*, Auszubildende(r) *(f⟨m⟩)*; apprentices' (training) shop: Lehrwerkstatt *(f)*; apprentice's certificate: Lehrzeugnis *(n)*; apprentices' (final) examination: Gesellenprüfung *(f)*.

apprenticeable occupation — Lehrberuf *(m)*.

apprenticeship — Ausbildung *(f)*, Lehre *(f)*; articles of apprenticeship: Lehrvertrag *(m)*.

approve *(v)* — zustimmen, genehmigen.

arbiter *⟨AE⟩* — Schlichter(in) *(m ⟨f⟩)*, Schiedsmann *(m)*, Berufungsrichter(in) *(m ⟨f⟩)*.

arbitral award — Schiedsspruch *(m)*.

arbitration — Schlichtung *(f)*, Schiedsspruch *(m)*; arbitration agreement: Schiedsabkommen *(n)*; arbitration board: Schiedsstelle *(f)*; arbitration committee: Schlichtungsstelle *(f)*, Vermittlungsausschuß *(m)*.

arbitrator — Schlichter(in) *(m ⟨f⟩)*, Vermittler(in) *(m ⟨f⟩)*

area — Bereich *(m)*, Gebiet *(n)*; area of competence: Geltungsbereich *(m)* *⟨sachlicher⟩*; area of operation: Geschäftsbereich *(m)*; area of responsibility: Verantwortungsbereich *(m)*.

armed forces — Wehrmacht *(f)*, Streitkräfte *(f, Pl)*.

army — Heer *(n)*.

articles of apprenticeship — Lehrvertrag *(m)*.

assembly — Versammlung *(f)*, Montage *(f)*; assembly line: Montageband *(n)*, Fließband *(n)*; assembly line production: Fließbandfertigung *(f)* /-montage *(f)*; assembly operation/shop: Montagebetrieb *(m)*; assembly work: Montagearbeit *(f)*.

assessment — Bewertung *(f)*, Einschätzung *(f)*; basis for assessment: Bemessungsgrundlage *(f)*.

assessor — Beisitzer *(m)*.

assign *(v)* — zuweisen, zuteilen.

assignment — Aufgabenzuweisung *(f)*, Aufgabe *(f)*; assignment of labo(u)r: Einsatz *(m)* von Personal.

assist *(v)* — mitarbeiten, helfen, unterstützen.

assistance — Mitarbeit *(f)*, Mitwirkung *(f)*, Hilfe *(f)*, Unterstützung *(f)*; in need of assistance: hilfsbedürftig.

assistant — Gehilfe *(m)*, Gehilfin *(f)*; clerical assistant: Bürogehilfe *(m)*, Bürogehilfin *(f)*.

associate — Berufs-/Standeskollege *(m)*; associate judge: Beisitzer(in) *(m ⟨f⟩)* bei Gericht.

assumption of office — Dienstantritt *(m)*.

atmosphere at work — Betriebsklima *(n)*.

attachment — Pfändung *(f)*. Beschlagnahme *(f)*.

attempt at conciliation/mediation — Schlichtungsversuch *(m)*.

attendance — Anwesenheit *(f)*; attendance fee: Sitzungsgeld *(n)*, Diäten *(Pl)*; attendance time: Wartezeit *(f)*, *⟨Zeitstudie⟩*.

attestation — Bescheinigung *(f)*, Zeugnis *(n)*.

auditor — Revisor(in) *(m ⟨f⟩)*, Buchprüfer(in) *(m ⟨f⟩)*.

authoritative *(adj)* — kompetent.

authority — Fachmann *(m)*, Kapazität *(f)*, Vollmacht *(f)*; authority to act: Handlungsvollmacht *(f)*; authority to negotiate: Abschlußvollmacht *(f)*; authority to sign: Unterschriftsvollmacht *(f)*.

authorize *(v)* — bevollmächtigen, ermächtigen; authorized clerk: Prokurist(in) *(m ⟨f⟩)*; authorized proxy/agent: Prozeßbevollmächtigte(r) *(f ⟨m⟩)*; authorized to sign: zeichnungsberechtigt.

automobile mechanic — Kraftfahrzeugschlosser *(m)*.

autonomy in negotiating wage rates — Tarifautonomie *(f)*.

auxiliary *(adj)* — zusätzlich, helfend; auxiliary establishment: Nebenbetrieb *(m)*; auxiliary personnel: Hilfspersonal *(n)*; auxiliary worker: Hilfsarbeiter(in) *(m ⟨f⟩)*.

avocation — Nebenberuf *(m)*.

avocational *(adj)* — nebenberuflich.

avoidance — Anfechtung *(f)*.

award — Auszeichnung *(f)*, Belohnung *(f)*, Prämie *(f)*, Preis *(m)*.

award *(v)* **a bonus/premium for** — etw. prämi(i)eren.

award *(v)* **a prize to** — jmd. prämi(i)eren.

B

Bachelor of Commerce *⟨BE⟩* — Diplomkaufmann *(m)*, Diplomkauffrau *(f)*.

balance sheet — Bilanz *(f)*, *⟨Unterlage⟩*.

ballot — *⟨geheime⟩* Wahl *(f)*, Wahlgang *(m)*, Gesamtzahl *(f)* der abgegebenen Stimmen; additional ballot: Stichentscheid *(m)*, Stichwahl *(f)*; postal ballot: Briefwahl *(f)*; ballot paper: Stimmzettel *(m)*.

ba(u)lk *(v)* — streiken, sich sträuben, etw. verhindern.

ban — Verbot *(n)*, Sperre *(f)*, Ablehnung *(f)*; ban on strikes: Streikverbot *(n)*; overtime ban: Überstundensperre *(f)*.

bandwork — Gruppenarbeit *(f)*.

bankruptcy — Konkurs *(m)*.

bargain *(v) (for)* — (etwas) aushandeln.

bargaining (on, about) — Verhandlung *(f)* (über).

bargaining agreement — Tarifabkommen *(n)*.

barred *(adj)* — abgesperrt, verriegelt; be

barred by the statute of limitations: verjähren.

base rate — Grundtarif *(m)*.

base time — Normalarbeitszeit *(f)*.

base wage — Grundlohn *(m)*.

basic *(adj)* — grundlegend; basic income: Grundeinkommen *(n)*; Basic Law for the Federal Republic of Germany: Grundgesetz *(n)* für die Bundesrepublik Deutschland; basic rate: Grundtarif *(m)*; basic regulation/rule: Rahmenbestimmung *(f)*; basic right (of a citizen): Grundrecht *(n)*; basic skills *(Pl)*: Grundfertigkeiten *(f, Pl)*, basic study: Grundstudium *(n)*; basic training: Grundausbildung *(f)*; basic wage: Grundlohn *(m)*.

basis — Grundlage *(f)*; basis for assessment: Bemessungsgrundlage *(f)*; basis for calculation: Berechnungsgrundlage *(f)*.

behavio(u)ral science — Verhaltenswissenschaft *(f)*.

better o. s. *(v)* — sich finanziell verbessern, vorwärtskommen.

blackleg *(v)* ⟨*BE*⟩ — gegen die Gewerkschaftssatzungen verstoßen.

blackleg ⟨*BE*⟩ ⟨*colloq*⟩ — Streikbrecher *(m)*; blackleg work: Streikarbeit *(f)*.

blue-collar worker ⟨*AE*⟩ — gewerbliche(r) Arbeitnehmer(in) *(m* ⟨*f*⟩*)*.

board of supervision — Aufsichtsrat *(m)*.

board of trade ⟨*AE*⟩ — Handelskammer *(f)*.

bodily *(adj)* — körperlich, physisch, leiblich.

bona fide *(adj)* — gutgläubig.

bonus — Gratifikation *(f)*, Tantieme *(f)*, Sondervergütung *(f)*, Zuschlag *(m)*, Prämie *(f)*.

bookdealer — Buchhändler(in) *(m* ⟨*f*⟩*)*.

bookkeeper — Buchhalter(in) *(m* ⟨*f*⟩*)*.

bookkeeping clerk — Buchhalter(in) *(m* ⟨*f*⟩*)*.

bookseller — Buchhändler(in) *(m* ⟨*f*⟩*)*.

boom — Hochkonjunktur *(f)*.

boss — Chef(in) *(m* ⟨*f*⟩*)*.

bottom pay rate — Niedriglohn *(m)*.

bracket — Schicht *(f)* ⟨*Gruppe von Arbeitern*⟩.

brainstorming — Ideenfindung *(f)*.

branch of production — Produktionszweig *(m)*.

breach of duty — Pflichtverletzung *(f)*.

bread ticket — Essenbon *(m)*, Essen-

marke *(f)*.

break — Pause *(f)*, Arbeitspause *(f)*; break-room: Pausenraum *(m)*.

breakdown — Zusammenbruch *(m)*, Aufgliederung *(f)*, Scheitern *(n)*, Aufteilung *(f)*, Betriebsausfall *(m)*.

brief *(v)* — einweisen, unterweisen.

broken *(adj)* — kaputt.

buddy ⟨*colloq*⟩ — Pate *(m)*, Anlerner *(m)*.

building loan — Baudarlehen *(n)*.

bulletin — ⟨*formeller*⟩ Aushang *(m)*; bulletin board: Aushangbrett *(n)*, Schwarzes Brett *(n)*.

bump *(v)* — bei der sozialen Auswahlen andere Arbeitnehmer verdrängen.

Bureau of Labor Statistics ⟨*AE*⟩ — Statistisches Arbeitsamt *(n)*.

business — Aufgabe *(f)*, Betrieb *(m)*, Geschäft *(n)*, Pflicht *(f)*; on business: geschäftlich, dienstlich; business call: Dienstgespräch *(n)*; business cycle: Konjukturkreislauf *(m)*; business department: Betriebsabteilung *(f)*; business English: Handelsenglisch *(n)*; business failure: Konkurs *(m)*; business luncheon: Arbeitsessen *(n)*; business outlook/trend: Geschäftsaussichten *(f)*, Konjunkturverlauf *(m)*; business paper: Fachzeitschrift *(f)*; business report: Geschäftsbericht *(m)*; business school ⟨*AE*⟩: Handelsakademie *(f)*; business secret: Geschäftsgeheimnis *(f)*; business travel/trip: Geschäftsreise *(f)*, Dienstreise *(f)*.

bylaw — Satzung *(f)*, Statut *(n)*.

C

cafeteria — Kantine *(f)* für Erfrischungen.

call — Forderung *(f)*; subject to call: kündbar; call to strike: Streifaufruf *(m)*.

callable *(adj)* — kündbar.

cancel(l)ation clause — Kündigungsklausel *(f)*.

candidate — Bewerber(in) *(m ⟨f⟩)*; candidate for scholastic hono(u)rs: Doktorand(in) *(m ⟨f⟩)*.

canteen — Gemeinschaftsküche *(f)*, Kantine *(f)*; canteen facilities *(Pl)*: Kantineneinrichtung *(f)*; Kantinenausstattung *(f)*; canteen food: Kantinenessen *(n)*; canteen manager: Kantinenwirt *(m)*.

capability — Befähigung *(f)*.

capable *(adj)* — qualifiziert, fähig; capable of being developped: bildungsfähig ⟨*Geist*⟩; capable of being educated: bildungsfähig ⟨*Mensch*⟩; capable to sue and be sued: prozeßfähig.

capacity — Eignung *(f)*, Qualifikation *(f)*, Kapazität *(f)*; capacity to contract: Geschäftsfähigkeit *(f)*; capacity to work: Arbeitsfähigkeit *(f)*.

capital accumulation — Vermögensbildung *(f)*; Capital Accumulation Act ⟨*Act to encourage the accumulation of capital by employe(e)s*⟩: Vermögensbildungsgesetz *(n)*.

care — Betreuung *(f)*, Fürsorge *(f)*.

career — Laufbahn *(f)*, Karriere *(f)*; career opportunities *(Pl)*, Karriere-/Aufstiegsmöglichkeiten *(f, Pl)*; career planning: Karriereplanung *(f)*, qualitative Personalplanung *(f)*.

caretaking — Betreuung *(f)*.

case — Prozeß *(m)*, Prozeßsache *(f)*, Rechtsstreit *(m)*; case files/records *(Pl)*: Prozeßakten *(f, Pl)*.

cash — Bargeld *(n)*; cash coefficient ⟨*price per time unit*⟩: Geldfaktor *(m)* ⟨*Akkordbezahlung*⟩; cash payment: Barzahlung *(f)*.

cashless *(adj)* — bargeldlos.

casting vote — Stichentscheid *(m)*, die entscheidende Stimme beim Stichentscheid.

catering department — Werkskantine *(f)*.

cause for recission — Anfechtungsgrund *(m)*.

causes *(Pl)* **for accident** — Unfallursachen *(f, Pl)*.

censure — Verweis *(m)*, Rüge *(f)*, Tadel *(m)*.

central *(adj)* — zentral; central department: Hauptabteilung *(f)*; central office: Hauptverwaltung *(f)*; central works council: Gesamtbetriebsrat *(m)*.

certificate — Zeugnis *(m)*; certificate of apprenticeship: Lehrzeugnis *(n)*, Gesellenbrief *(m)*; certificate of character: Führungszeugnis *(n)*; certificate of disability: Arbeitsunfähigkeitsbescheinigung *(f)*; certificate of discharge: Entlassungszeugnis *(n)*; certificate of employment: Beschäftigungsnachweis *(m)*; certificate of good behavio(u)r: Leumundszeugnis *(n)*.

certification — Bescheinigung *(f)*.

certified engineer — Diplomingenieur *(m)*.

chamber of commerce — Handelskammer *(f)*.

Chamber of Industry and Commerce — Industrie- und Handelskammer *(f)*.

change in the personnel/staff — Personalwechsel *(m)*.

change of shift — Schichtwechsel *(m)*.

changing room — Umkleideraum *(m)*.

character — Charakter *(m)*, Leumund *(m)*, Führungszeugnis *(n)* für Angestellte.

charges *(Pl)* — Spesen *(f)*, Gebühren *(f)*.

charitable *(adj)* — gemeinnützig.

check off ⟨AE⟩ — Einbehaltung (f) von Gewerkschaftsbeiträgen.

chief — Leiter(in) (m ⟨f⟩), Chef(in) (m ⟨f⟩); chief clerk: Bürovorsteher(in) (m ⟨f⟩); chief engineer: Oberingenieur(in) (m ⟨f⟩); chief of personnel: Personalchef(in) (m ⟨f⟩).

child bounty ⟨AE⟩ — Kinderzulage (f).

child welfare worker — Jugendpfleger(in) (m ⟨f⟩).

children's allowance — Kindergeld (n).

Christmas bonus — Weihnachtsgeld (n), Weihnachtsgratifikation (f).

circular (letter) — Rundschreiben (n).

civil service ⟨BE⟩ — Staatsdienst (m).

claim — Forderung (f), Anspruch (m); have (v) a claim: anspruchsberechtigt sein; claim for damages: Schadenersatzforderung (f).

claimant — Beschwerdeführer (m), Kläger (m).

claims department/office — Schadensabteilung (f).

classification — Eingruppierung (f), Einstufung (f).

classify (v) — eingruppieren.

clearance card — Abgangszeugnis (n).

clerical assistant — Bürogehilfe (m), Bürogehilfin (f).

clerk — kaufm. Angestellte(r) (f ⟨m⟩), Sekretär(in) (m ⟨f⟩), Schreibkraft (f).

clock in/out (v) — ⟨Kontrolluhr⟩ stempeln.

close down (v) — Betrieb stillegen.

close of work — Arbeitsschluß (m).

closed shop — Betrieb, in dem nur Gewerkschaftsmitglieder tätig sind.

closure — Abschluß (m) einer Debatte, Stillegung (f) eines Betriebes.

co-decision — Mitbestimmung (f), Mitentscheid (m).

co-determination — Mitbestimmung (f); Co-determination Act: Mitbestimmungsgesetz (n).

co-determine (v) — mitbestimmen.

Code of Commerce — Handelsgesetzbuch (n).

code of procedure — Prozeßordnung (f).

collaborate (on) (v) — mitarbeiten (an, bei), zusammenarbeiten.

collaboration — Mitarbeit (f), Zusammenarbeit (f).

colleague — Arbeitskollege (m), Arbeitskollegin (f), Mitarbeiter(in) (m ⟨f⟩).

collection of signatures — Unterschriftensammlung (f).

collective (adj) — gesamt, gemeinschaftlich; collective agreement: Kollektivvertrag (m), Gesamtvereinbarung (f); Collective Agreements Act: Tarifvertragsgesetz (n); collective agreements area: Tarifbezirk (m); collective bargaining: Tarifverhandlungen (f, Pl), Kollektiv(-vertrags)verhandlungen (f, Pl); collective bargaining agreement: Tarifvereinbarung (f); collective bargaining commission: Tarifkommission (f), Verhandlungskommission (f); collective bargaining round: Tarifrunde (f); collective framework agreement: Manteltarifvertrag (m); collective labo(u)r agreement: Kollektivarbeitsvertrag (m); collective scale salary: Tarifgehalt (n); collective wage formation: Tarifgestaltung (f).

co-management — Mitbestimmung (f); Co-management Act: Mitbestimmungsgesetz (n) für die Montanindustrie.

commencement of work — Arbeitsbeginn (m).

commendatory letter — Empfehlungsschreiben (n).

commercial (adj) — geschäftlich, kaufmännisch; commercial agent: Handelsvertreter(in) (m ⟨f⟩); Commercial Code: Handelsgesetzbuch (n); Commercial Court: Handelsgericht (n); commercial law: Handelsrecht (n); in accordance with commercial law: handelsrechtlich; commercial register: Handelsregister (n); commercial school: Handelsschule (f); commercial travel(l)er: Handelsreisender (m).

commissary — Kantine (f), Verpflegungsausgabe (f).

commission — Provision (f); commission for collective wage agreements: Tarifkommission (f) für Lohnverhandlungen; commission rate: Provisionssatz (m).

committee (on) — Ausschuß (m) (für).

common work — Handarbeit (f).

commute (v) — pendeln (zwischen Wohnung und Arbeitsstätte).

commuter ⟨AE⟩ — Pendler(in) (m ⟨f⟩).

company — Firma (f), Unternehmen (n); company agreement: Haustarif(vertrag) (m); company anniversary: Firmenjubiläum (n); company consultant: Betriebsberater(in) (m ⟨f⟩); company doctor/physician: Betriebsarzt (m), Betriebsärztin (f); company flat: Dienstwohnung (f); company magazine: Werkszeitung (f), Betriebszeitschrift (f); company owned/sponsored housing (for employees): Werkswohnung (f); company pension: Betriebsrente (f); company pension scheme: betriebliche Altersversorgung (f); company saving plan/system: betriebliche Sparförderung (f); company time: bezahlte Arbeitszeit (f).

compassionate leave — Sonderurlaub (m) ⟨bei Trauerfall etc.⟩.

compensate (v) ⟨AE⟩ — entlohnen, entschädigen.

compensation — Entlohnung (f), Entgelt (n), Entschädigung (f), Vergütung (f), Wiedergutmachung (f); compensation for services (rendered): Leistungsausgleich (m); compensation for wage deficiencies (Pl): Lohnausgleich (m); compensation for wages/pay/earnings lost: Entschädigung (f) für Lohnverlust, Lohnausgleich (f); compensation package: Gesamtvergütung (f).

competency — Zuständigkeit (f).

competent (adj) — zuständig, kompetent.

competition clause — Wettbewerbsklausel (f), Konkurrenzklausel (f).

competitive examination — Ausleseprüfung (f).

competitor — Mitbewerber(in) (m ⟨f⟩).

complainer — Beschwerdeführer(in) (m ⟨f⟩).

complaint — Beschwerde (f), Klage (f); subject of complaint: Beschwerdepunkt (m).

complete (v) one's apprenticeship — auslernen.

completion of one's education — Ausbildungsabschluß (m).

composition — Vergleich (m), mit Gläubiger; composition payment: Ablösezahlung (f).

comprehensive school ⟨BE⟩ — Gesamtschule (f).

compromise — Vergleich (m).

compulsory (adj) — obligatorisch, zwangsweise; compulsory arbitration: Zwangsschlichtung (f); compulsory contribution: Pflicht-/Zwangsbeitrag (m); compulsory insurance: Pflichtversicherung (f).

conceal (v) fraudently — arglistig verschweigen.

conciliation — Vermittlung (f); conciliation committee: Einigungsstelle *(f)*; conciliation proceedings *(Pl)*: Vermittlungs-/Einigungsverfahren *(n)*.

conclusion — Abschluß *(m)*.

concurrence — Genehmigung *(f)*.

conduct *(v)* — führen, leiten.

confer *(v)* **a (doctor's) degree up(on)** — promovieren.

confidential *(adj)* — vertraulich; confidential post: Vertrauensstellung *(f)*.

confirmation — Bestätigung *(f)*.

conscientious objector — Kriegsdienstverweigerer *(m)*.

conscription order — Einberufungsbefehl *(m)* ⟨mil⟩.

consent — Zustimmung *(f)*, Einverständnis *(n)*; by mutual consent: im gegenseitigen Einverständnis *(n)*, einvernehmlich.

constitution — Verfassung *(f)*, Grundgesetz *(n)*.

constitutional right — Grundrecht *(n)*.

constructor — Konstrukteur *(m)*.

consultation hour — Sprechstunde *(f)*.

contestation — Anfechtung *(f)*.

contesting of an election — Wahlanfechtung *(f)*.

continuation course — Fortbildungslehrgang *(m)*.

continuation of payments (to sick workers) — Lohnfortzahlung *(f)* im Krankheitsfall.

contract — Vertrag *(m)*; contract - breaking *(adj)*: vertragsbrüchig; contract for work and service: Werkvertrag *(m)*; contract system: Gedinge *(n)*; contract wage payment: Akkordsatz *(m)*, Akkordbezahlung *(f)*.

contracting out — Vergabe *(f)* von Arbeiten nach außerhalb.

contractual *(adj)* — vertraglich; contractual penalty: Vertragsstrafe *(f)*; contractual power: Abschlußvollmacht *(f)*; contractual relationship: Vertragsverhältnis; contract wage(s): Tariflohn *(m)*.

contribution to the pension scheme — Pensionsbeitrag *(m)*.

control — Aufsicht *(f)*, Überprüfung *(f)*.

controller — Rechnungsprüfer(in) *(m ⟨f⟩)*.

convalescence — Erholung *(f)* von einer Krankheit.

cooling-off period — Abkühlungsphase *(f)*.

cooperation — Mitarbeit *(f)*, Mitwirkung *(f)*.

copy of a certificate/diploma — Zeugnisabschrift *(f)*.

core time — Kernarbeitszeit *(f)*.

corrective training — Entziehungskur *(f)*.

correspondence — Übereinstimmung *(f)*, Briefwechsel *(m)*; correspondence course: Fernlehrgang *(m)*; correspondence lesson: Lehrbrief *(m)* eines Fernlehrgangs; correspondence school/college: Fernlehrinstitut *(n)*.

cost — Kosten *(Pl)*, Spesen *(Pl)*; cost accounting: Betriebsbuchhaltung *(f)*; cost-conscious *(adj)*: kostenbewußt; cost cut: Kostenabbau *(m)*; cost-cutting drive: Sparprogramm *(n)*; cost for an action/lawsuit: Prozeßkosten *(Pl)*; cost of living: Lebenshaltungskosten *(Pl)*; cost of living allowance: Lebenshaltungskosten-Ausgleich *(m)*, Teuerungszuschlag *(m)*; cost of production: Fertigungskosten *(Pl)*; cost reduction: Kostenreduzierung *(f)*.

course — Lehrgang *(n)*, Kursus *(m)*.

court of hono(u)r — Ehrengericht *(n)*.

court of trade — Handelskammer *(f)*.

court rules *(Pl)* — Prozeßordnung *(f)*.

coverage — *⟨sachl.⟩* Geltungsbereich *(m)*.

co-worker — Arbeitskollege *(m)*, Arbeitskollegin *(f)*.

crackdown *⟨AE⟩* — Maßregelung *(f)*.

craft — Beruf *(m)*, Handwerk *(n)*, Geschicklichkeit *(f)*.

craftmaster — Handwerksmeister *(m)*.

craftsman — *⟨gelernter⟩* Handwerker *(m)*.

craftsmanship — handwerkliches Können.

credential — Leumundszeugnis *(n)*, Empfehlungsschreiben *(n)*.

criminal report — Vorstrafenregister *(n)*.

cry off *(v)* — absagen, zurücktreten.

cultivable *(adj)* — bildungsfähig.

culture — Bildung *(f)*.

curator — Pfleger(in) *(m ⟨f⟩)* für Entmündigte.

curriculum vitae — *⟨geschriebener⟩* Lebenslauf *(m)*.

custody — Haft *(f)*.

customary right — Gewohnheitsrecht *(n)*.

cut in pay/wages — Lohnkürzung *(f)*, Lohnsenkung *(f)*.

cutback in manpower — Arbeitskräfteabbau *(m)*.

cycle time — Taktzeit *(f)*.

D

daily breader *⟨BE⟩* — Pendler(in) *(m ⟨f⟩)*.

damage to s.one's health — Gesundheitsschaden *(m)*.

danger allowance — Gefahrenzulage *(f)*.

data — Daten *(Pl)*; data processing: Datenverarbeitung *(f)*; data protection: Datenschutz *(m)*; data protection representative: Datenschutzbeauftragter *(m)*.

day off for women with own household — Hausarbeitstag *(m)*.

deadline — Befristung *(f)*, Stichtag *(m)*, letzter Termin *(m)*.

deadline s. th. *(v)* — etwas befristen.

death benefit — Hinterbliebenenrente *(f)*, Sterbegeld *(n)*.

decision making — Entscheidungsfindung *(f)*.

decline in performance — Leistungsabfall *(m)*.

decrease in production — Produktionsrückgang *(m)*.

decree — Verordnung *(f)*, Verfügung *(f)*; decree of forthcoming writ of attachment: Pfändungs- und Überweisungsbeschluß *(n)*.

deduction — Einbehaltung *(f)* (von Steuern); deduction of union dues: Einbehaltung *(f)* von Gewerkschaftsbeiträgen; deduction of wage(s') tax: Lohnsteuerabzug *(m)*; deduction(s) from wages/pay: Lohnabzug *(m)*.

defamatory *(adj)* — ehrenrührig.

degree — Grad *(m)*.

delay — (Arbeits-)Verzögerung *(f)*.

delegate *(v)* — delegieren.

demand — Forderung *(f)*, Anspruch *(m)*; demand for employees/workers: Arbeitskräftebedarf *(m)*.

department — Abteilung *(f)* ⟨*eines Betriebes*⟩; department manager: Abteilungsleiter *(m)*; Department of Labor ⟨*AE*⟩ — Arbeitsministerium *(n)*; department(al) head: Abteilungsleiter(in) *(m ⟨f⟩)*; department(al) meeting: Abteilungsversammlung *(f)*.

dependency bonus/allowance — Kinderzulage *(f)*.

dependent *(adj)* — unselbständig, abhängig.

depreciation — Wertminderung *(f)*, Abschreibung *(f)*.

deputy — ⟨*amtliche(r)*⟩ Stellvertreter(in) *(m ⟨f⟩)*; deputy member: Ersatzmitglied *(n)*.

design engineer — Konstrukteur(in) *(m ⟨f⟩)*.

detention — Haft *(f)*.

detrimental *(adj)* **to health** — gesundheitsschädlich, gesundheitsschädigend.

development of wages/pay — Lohnentwicklung *(f)*.

differentiation of wage(s) — Lohnstaffelung *(f)*.

diploma ⟨*AE*⟩ — Diplom *(n)*, Abgangszeugnis *(n)*, Prüfungszeugnis *(n)*.

direct *(v)* — anordnen, anweisen, (Betrieb) leiten.

direct labo(u)r cost — Fertigungslöhne *(m, Pl)*.

direct union agreement — Haustarif(vertrag) *(m)*.

direction — Anordnung *(f)*, Weisung *(f)*, Verfügung *(f)*; subject to directions *(Pl)* — weisungsgebunden.

directors' fees — Aufsichtsratsvergütung *(f)*.

disability — Berufsunfähigkeit *(f)*, Arbeitsunfähigkeit *(f)*, Behinderung *(f)*, Invalidität *(f)*.

disabled *(adj)* — berufsunfähig, behindert, arbeitsunfähig; -permanently disabled: erwerbsunfähig; Disabled Persons Act ⟨*Act respecting the employment of disabled persons*⟩: Schwerbehindertengesetz *(n)*; disabled persons representative: Vertrauensmann *(m)* der Schwerbehinderten.

disablement — Erwerbsunfähigkeit *(f)*, Invalidität *(f)*; disablement annuity: Invaliditätsrente *(f)*.

discharge *(v)* — entlassen.

discharge — Entlassung *(f)*; discharge paper: Arbeitsbescheinigung *(f)*.

disciplinary *(adj)* — disziplinarisch, erzieherisch; disciplinary case: Disziplinarfall *(m)*; disciplinary penalty/punishment: Disziplinarstrafe *(f)*; disciplinary procedures: Disziplinarbestimmungen *(f, Pl)*; disciplinary punishment: Maßregelung *(f)*; disciplinary transfer: Strafversetzung *(f)*.

discount — Skonto *(n)*, Rabatt *(m)*.

discreditable *(adj)* — ehrenrührig.

discretion — Verschwiegenheit *(f)*.

discrimination — Benachteiligung *(f)*.

dislocate *(v)* — umsetzen ⟨*Arbeitskräfte*⟩.

dismiss *(v)* — entlassen.

dismissal — Entlassung *(f)*, Kündigung *(f)* ⟨*durch Arbeitgeber*⟩; dismissal compensation: Entlassungsentschädigung *(f)*; dismissal pay: Entlassungsgeld *(n)*.

displaced person — Zwangsarbeiter *(m)*.

displacement — Versetzung *(f)*.

disposition — Verfügung *(f)*.

dispute machinery — Schlichtungsverfahren *(n)*.

disqualification — Unfähigkeit *(f)*, Untauglichkeit *(f)*.

dissuasion — Abmahnung *(f)*.

distrainment — Pfändung *(f)*.

distress — Pfändung *(f)*.

distribution of wage costs — Lohnkostenverteilung *(f)*.

division — Abteilung *(f)* einer Verwaltung; division of labo(u)r: Arbeitsteilung *(f)*.

docker ⟨*BE*⟩ — Hafenarbeiter *(m)*.

doctor's certificate — Attest *(n)*, ärztliches Zeugnis *(n)*.

doctor's degree — Doktortitel *(m)*.

doctoral candidate — Doktorand(in) *(m ⟨f⟩)*.

doctoral thesis/dissertation — Doktorarbeit *(f)*.

doctorand — Doktorand(in) *(m ⟨f⟩)*.

doctorate — Doktortitel *(m)*.

dodging *(adj)* ⟨*BE*⟩ — arbeitsscheu.

doing — Tätigkeit *(f)*, Handeln *(n)*.

domestic *(adj)* — häuslich, inländisch; domestic science: Hauswirtschaftslehre *(f)*; domestic science college: Haushaltungsschule *(f)*; domestic servant:

Hausangestellte(r) *(f ⟨m⟩)*.

dominant leader — Führungspersönlichkeit *(f)*.

done in good faith *(adj)* — gutgläubig gehandelt.

doorkeeper — Pförtner(in) *(m ⟨f⟩)*.

downtime — Ausfallzeit *(f)*, Arbeitsausfall *(m)*.

downing tools — Arbeitsniederlegung *(f)*.

downswing — Konjunkturabschwächung *(f)*.

downward trend in the business cycle — Konjunkturabschwächung *(f)*.

draft order ⟨*AE*⟩ — Einberufungsbefehl *(m)* ⟨*mil*⟩.

draftee — Wehrpflichtiger *(m)*.

driver — Kraftfahrer *(m)*.

dry-out — Entziehungskur *(f)*.

due for retirement ⟨*colloq*⟩ — pensionsreif.

duties *(Pl)* — Aufgabenbereich *(m)*.

duty — Pflicht *(f)*, Aufgabe *(f)*, Dienst *(m)*; duty of notification: Meldepflicht *(f)* ⟨*bei Krankheit*⟩; duty to report: Anzeigepflicht *(f)*.

E

eagerness for/to work — Arbeitseifer *(m)*.

earned income — Arbeitseinkommen *(n)*; earned income allowance: Arbeitnehmerfreibetrag *(m)*.

earnings *(Pl)* — Verdienst *(m)*, Erträge *(Pl)*, Einkommen *(n)*; earnings level: Lohnniveau *(n)*; earnings lost: Verdienstausfall *(m)*.

economic *(adj)* — wirtschaftlich, ratio-

nell; economic aid: Wirtschaftshilfe *(f)*; economic committee: Wirtschaftsausschuß *(m)*; economic cycle: Konjunkturkreislauf *(m)*; economic situation/ activity: Wirtschaftslage *(f)*; economic trend: Konjunktur *(f)*.

educ(at)able *(adj)* — bildungsfähig.

education — Ausbildung *(f)*, Erziehung *(f)*; classical education: humanistische Bildung *(f)*; education subsidy/allowance: Erziehungsbeihilfe *(f)*.

educational *(adj)* — erzieherisch, pädagogisch; education(al) grant: Ausbildungsbeihilfe *(f)*, Erziehungsbeihilfe *(f)*; educational background: Vorbildung *(f)*; educational channel: Bildungsweg *(m)*; educational leave: Bildungsurlaub *(m)*; educational level: Bildungsniveau *(n)*; educational opportunities *(Pl)*: Bildungschancen *(f, Pl)*.

efficiency — Leistungsergebnis *(n)*, Leistungskraft/-fähigkeit *(f)*; efficiency contest: Leistungswettbewerb *(m)*; efficiency level: Leistungsgrad *(m)*; efficiency rating: Leistungsbeurteilung *(f)*, Leistungsgradschätzung *(f)*; efficiency system: Leistungssystem *(n)*; efficiency payments *(Pl)*: Leistungsentgelt *(n)*.

efficient *(adj)* — leistungsfähig.

effort — Mühe *(f)*, Anstrengung *(f)*, Arbeit *(f)*.

eight-hour-day (8 hr day) — Achtstundentag *(m)*.

election — Wahl *(f)*; election campaign: Wahlkampf *(m)*; election contest: Wahlanfechtung *(f)*.

electoral board — Wahlvorstand *(m)*.

electrical engineer — Elektroingenieur(in) *(m ⟨f⟩)*.

electrician — Elektroinstallateur(in) *(m ⟨f⟩)*.

elementary education — Volksschulbildung *(f)*, Grundschulbildung *(f)*.

elementary school — Volksschule *(f)*, Grundschule *(f)*.

eligibility for a pension — Versorgungsanwartschaft *(f)*.

eligible *(adj)* — anspruchsberechtigt, wählbar; eligible for a pension: pensionsberechtigt.

emergency service — Notdienst *(m)*.

emoluments *(Pl)* — (besondere) Bezüge *(Pl)*, Nebeneinkünfte *(Pl)*, Diäten *(Pl)*, Tagegeld *(n)*.

employ *(v)* — beschäftigen, einstellen.

employability — Arbeitsfähigkeit *(f)*.

employed *(adj)* — beschäftigt, angestellt; employed person: Beschäftigte(r) *(f ⟨m⟩)*.

employe *⟨AE⟩*, **employee** *⟨BE⟩* — Arbeitnehmer(in) *(m ⟨f⟩)*, Betriebsangehörige(r) *(f ⟨m⟩)*, Beschäftigte(r) *(f ⟨m⟩)*; clerical employee: Büroangestellte(r) *(f ⟨m⟩)*; employee attitude survey: Betriebsumfrage *(f)*; employee benefit department: Sozialabteilung *(f)*; employee contribution: Arbeitnehmeranteil *(m)* zur Sozialversicherung; employee covered by/under collective agreement: Tarifangestellte(r) *(f ⟨m⟩)*; employee grievance: Beschwerdefall *(m)* ⟨*eines Arbeitnehmers*⟩; employee meeting: Betriebsversammlung *(f)*; employee moral: Arbeitsmoral *(f)*; employee rating *⟨AE⟩*: Einstufung *(f)*, Eingruppierung *(f)*; employee representation: Arbeitnehmervertretung *(f)*; employee representative: Arbeitnehmervertreter(in) *(m ⟨f⟩)*; employee roster: Stellenbesetzungsplan *(m)*; employee status: Anstellungsverhältnis *(n)*; employee suggestion scheme: (betriebliches) Vorschlagswesen *(n)*; employee turnover: (Arbeitskräfte-)Fluktuation *(f)*; employee invention: Arbeitnehmererfindung *(f)*; employee's withholding exemption: Lohnsteuerfreibetrag *(m)*; employees *(Pl)*: Personal *(n)*, Belegschaft *(f)*; employees' food services: Kantineneinrichtung *(f)*.

employer — Arbeitgeber *(m)*; employer contribution: Arbeitgeberanteil *(m)* zur Sozialversicherung; employer's duty for social care: Fürsorgepflicht *(f)*; Employer-Liability-Act *⟨AE⟩*: Arbeitgeber-Haftpflicht-Gesetz *(n)*; employers' liability insurance association: Berufs-genossenschaft *(f)*.

employment — Anstellung *(f)*, Arbeit *(f)*, Beschäftigung *(f)*, Tätigkeit *(f)*, Stellung *(f)*, Einsatz *(m)*; be in the employ(ment): beschäftigt sein; constant employment: Dauerbeschäftigung *(f)*; employment agency: Stellenvermittlung *(f)*; employment applicant: Arbeitssuchende(r) *(f ⟨m⟩)*, Bewerber(in) *(m ⟨f⟩)*; employment category: Beschäftigungsart *(f)*; employment certificate: Arbeitsbescheinigung *(f)*, Dienstzeugnis *(n)*; employment conditions *(Pl)*: Einstellungsbedingungen *(f, Pl)*, Beschäftigungsbedingungen *(f, Pl)*; employment conditions agreement: Manteltarifvertrag *(m)*; employment contract: Arbeits-/Dienstvertrag *(m)*; employment interview: Vorstellungsgespräch *(n)*; employment obligation: Beschäftigungspflicht *(f)*; employment of labo(u)r: Arbeitseinsatz *(m)*; employment on trial basis: Probearbeitsverhältnis *(n)*; employment papers: Arbeitspapiere *(n, Pl)*; Employment Promotion Act: Arbeitsförderungsgesetz *(n)*; employment relationship: Arbeitsverhältnis *(n)*, Dienstverhältnis *(n)*; employment scheme: Arbeitsbeschaffungsprogramm *(n)*; employment status: Dienststellung *(f)*; employment tax ⟨*AE*⟩: Lohnsteuer *(f)*.

end of work — Arbeitsschluß *(m)*.

engage *(v)* — einstellen.

engagement — Einstellung *(f)*, Anwerbung *(f)*.

engine fitter — Maschinenschlosser(in) *(m ⟨f⟩)*.

engineer — Ingenieur(in) *(m ⟨f⟩)*; certified engineer: Diplomingenieur(in) *(m ⟨f⟩)*.

enlist *(v)* — anwerben.

enlistment — Einstellung *(f)*, Anstellung *(f)*.

enrol(l)ment — Anmeldung *(f)* ⟨*zu einem Kursus*⟩.

enticement — Abwerbung *(f)* von Arbeitskräften.

entitle s.o. *(v)* — jmd. berechtigen, jmd. Anspruch geben auf; entitled to a pension: pensionsberechtigt; entitled to alimony: unterhaltsberechtigt ⟨*Ehefrau*⟩; entitled to maintenance: unterhaltsberechtigt ⟨*Kind*⟩; entitled to vote: wahlberechtigt, stimmberechtigt.

entitlement — Anspruch *(m)*; entitlement to a pension: Pensionsanspruch *(m)*.

entrance rate — Anfangslohn *(m)*, Anfangsgehalt *(n)*.

entry into service — Dienstantritt *(m)*.

environment(al) protection — Umweltschutz *(m)*.

environtent(al) protection representative — Umweltschutzbeauftragter *(m)*.

equal *(adj)* — gleich(wertig); equal opportunities *(Pl)*: Chancengleichheit *(f)*; equal rights *(Pl)* (for women): Gleichberechtigung *(f)* (der Frau); equal treatment: Gleichbehandlung *(f)*.

equality — Gleichheit *(f)*; equality in wages: Lohngleichheit *(f)*; equality of pay: Lohngleichheit *(f)*; equality of rights/status: Gleichberechtigung *(f)*.

equalization contribution/pay for non employment of disabled persons — Ausgleichsabgabe *(f)* nach dem Schwerbehindertengesetz.

equipment — Arbeitszeug *(n)*, Ausrüstung *(f)*.

ergonomic design — ergonomische Gestaltung *(f)*.

ergonomic science — Arbeitswissenschaft *(f)*.

ergonomics *(Pl)* — Arbeitswissenschaft *(f)*.

establishment — Betrieb *(m)*.

estimate of a person's character — Charakterbeurteilung *(f)* einer Person.

evening classes *(Pl)* — Abendkurs(us) *(m)*.

examination — Prüfung *(f)*; examination for the General Certificate of Education ⟨*BE*⟩ — Abitur *(n)*, Reifeprüfung *(f)*; examination for the master's diploma/certificate: Meisterprüfung *(f)*.

exclusivity stipulation ⟨*BE*⟩ — Wettbewerbsklausel *(f)*, Konkurrenzklausel *(f)*.

execute *(v)* — erledigen, ausführen.

executive *(adj)* — vollziehend, ausübend; executive ability: Führungseigenschaft *(f)*; executive board: Vorstand *(m)*; executive employee: Führungskraft *(f)*.

exempted amount — Pfändungsfreibetrag *(m)*.

exemption from social insurance — Sozialversicherungsfreiheit *(f)*.

exemption from work(ing) — Arbeitsbefreiung *(f)*.

exhaustion — Erschöpfung *(f)*.

exit control — Torkontrolle *(f)*, Ausgangskontrolle *(f)*.

expansion of production — Produktionssteigerung *(f)*, Produktionsausweitung *(f)*.

expectation — Anwartschaft *(f)*.

expense *(s)* — Kosten *(Pl)*, Ausgabe *(f)*, Auslagen *(f, Pl)*; expense allowance: Aufwandsentschädigung *(f)*; expense reimbursement: Auslagenerstattung *(f)*; expense account rules: Spesenrichtlinien *(f, Pl)*.

expert — Fachmann *(m)*; expert opinion: Gutachten *(n)*.

expertise survey — Gutachten *(n)*.

extra *(adj)* — besonders, außergewöhnlich, zusätzlich; extra allowance: Sondervergütung *(f)*, Sonderzuschlag *(m)*; extra charge/burden: Mehrbelastung *(f)*, Zuschlag *(m)*; extra hour: Überstunde *(f)*; extra leave: Sonderurlaub *(m)*; extra pay: Lohnzuschlag *(m)*, Prämie *(f)*, Gehaltszulage *(f)*, Zusatzlohn *(m)*; extra work: Mehrarbeit *(f)*.

F

face guard — Schutzmaske *(f)*.

face shield — Schutzschild *(m)* ⟨*bei Schweißarbeiten*⟩.

factory — Betriebsanlage *(f)*, Fabrik *(f)*; Factory Act ⟨*BE*⟩: Arbeitsschutzgesetz *(n)*; factory meeting: Betriebsversammlung *(f)*; factory worker: Fabrikarbeiter(in) *(m* ⟨*f*⟩*)*, Industriearbeiter(in) *(m* ⟨*f*⟩*)*.

faculty — Können *(n)*.

fail *(v)* **in an examination** — im Examen durchfallen.

failure — Scheitern *(n)*, Mißlingen *(n)*.

fall in production — Produktionsrückgang *(m)*.

falling off in output — Produktionsrückgang *(m)*.

familiarize *(v)* **o.s. with** — sich einarbeiten.

family allowance — Kindergeld *(n)*, Familienbeihilfe *(f)*.

family care — Familienfürsorge *(f)*.

fatigue allowance — Erholungszuschlag *(m)*, Ermüdungszuschlag *(m)*.

Federal Constitutional Court — Bundesverfassungsgericht *(n)*.

Federal Data Protection Act ⟨*Act on protection against the misuse of personal data in data processing*⟩ — Bundesdatenschutzgesetz *(n)*.

Federal Employment Institution — Bundesanstalt für Arbeit *(f)*.

Federal Family Allowance Act ⟨*Act respecting the grant of family and education supplement*⟩ — Bundeskindergeldgesetz *(n)*.

Federal Finance Court — Bundesfinanzhof *(m)*.

Federal Gazette — Bundesgesetzblatt *(n)*.

Federal Labo(u)r Court — Bundesarbeitsgericht *(n)*.

Federal Leave Act ⟨*Act to provide for a minimum period of leave for workers*⟩ — Bundesurlaubsgesetz *(n)*.

Federal Minister of Labo(u)r — Bundesarbeitsminister *(m)*.

Federal Social Insurance Institution for (Salaried) Employees — Bundesversicherungsanstalt *(f)* für Angestellte.

federal unemployment tax ⟨*AE*⟩ — Arbeitnehmerbeitrag *(m)* zur Arbeitslosenversicherung.

Federation of German Industries — Bundesverband *(m)* der Deutschen Industrie (BDI).

Federation of German Trade Unions — Deutscher Gewerkschaftsbund (DGB).

federation of industries *(Pl)* — Industrieverband *(m)*.

Federation of the German Employers' Associations — Bundesvereinigung *(f)* der Deutschen Arbeitgeberverbände (BDA).

fee — Honorar *(n)*, Vergütung *(f)*.

fees *(Pl)* — Gebühren *(f, Pl)*, Kosten *(Pl)*.

fellow worker — Arbeitskollege *(m)*, Arbeitskollegin *(f)*.

female occupation — Frauenarbeit *(f)*.

field — Arbeitsgebiet *(n)*; field of activity: Tätigkeitsbereich *(m)*.

file clerc ⟨*AE*⟩/filing clerc ⟨*BE*⟩ — Registrator(in) *(m* ⟨*f*⟩*)*.

final assembly — Fertigmontage *(f)*.

financial *(adj)* — finanziell; financial assistance to the gifted: Begabtenförderung *(f)*; financial strength: wirtschaftl. Leistungskraft; financially strong *(adj)*: kapitalkräftig, (wirtschaftlich) leistungsfähig.

finding of employment — Arbeitsvermittlung *(f)*.

findings *(Pl)* **of ergonomics** — arbeitswissenschaftliche Erkenntnisse *(f, Pl)*.

finish *(v)* — erledigen, beenden.

finish *(v)* **learning** — auslernen.

fire *(v)* ⟨*AE*⟩ — jdm. entlassen.

firm — Firma *(f)*, Betrieb *(m)*.

fit for work *(adj)* — arbeitsfähig.

fitness — Befähigung *(f)*, Eignung *(f)*, Qualifikation *(f)*; fitness test: Eignungsuntersuchung *(f)* ⟨*med*⟩.

fitter — Schlosser(in) *(m* ⟨*f*⟩*)*.

fix up *(v)* — erledigen.

fixed costs *(Pl)* — Gemeinkosten *(Pl)*.

flat ⟨*BE*⟩ — Mietwohnung *(f)*.

flat *(adj)* — flach, eben, glatt, seicht; flat charge (rate): Pauschale *(f)*; flat rate: Grundlohn *(m)*.

fleet works council — Seebetriebsrat *(m)*.

flextime — flexible Arbeitszeit *(f)*.

flop — Versager *(m)*.

flow chart — Arbeitsablaufplan *(m)*.

fluctuation — Fluktuation *(f)*.

flunk *(v)* **in an examination** ⟨*AE*⟩ — im Examen durchfallen.

foreign worker/labo(u)r — Fremdarbeiter(in) *(m ⟨f⟩)*, ausländ. Arbeitnehmer(in) *(m ⟨f⟩)*.

forelady — Betriebsmeisterin *(f)*.

foreman — Betriebsmeister *(m)*.

forewoman — Betriebsmeisterin *(f)*.

forfeiture — Verwirkung *(f)*.

formal education — Bildung *(f)*.

formation of a coalition — Koalitionsbildung *(f)*.

framework law — Rahmengesetz *(n)*.

free *(adj)* — arbeitsfrei.

freedom of association — Koalitionsfreiheit *(f)*.

freedom to strike — Streikrecht *(n)*.

fringe benefits *(Pl)* ⟨AE⟩ — Lohnnebenleistungen *(f, Pl)*, Sozialgemeinkosten *(Pl)*.

frontier worker — Grenzgänger *(m)*.

full employment — Vollbeschäftigung *(f)*.

full legal age (for) — Geschäftsfähigkeit *(f)*.

full-time *(adj)* — hauptamtlich, ganztägig; full-time employment: Ganztagsbeschäftigung *(f)*.

function — Geschäftsbereich *(m)*, Aufgabenbereich *(m)*, Aufgabe *(f)*, Pflicht *(f)*.

functional *(adj)* — fachlich.

fundamental right — Grundrecht *(n)*.

further education/training — Fortbildung *(f)*.

G

gainful activity — Gewerbetätigkeit *(f)*.

gainfully employed *(adj)* — erwerbstätig.

garnishment of wages — Lohnpfändung *(f)*.

gate control — Torkontrolle *(f)*.

gatekeeper — Pförtner(in) *(m ⟨f⟩)*.

gear — Arbeitszeug *(n)*.

general *(adj)* — allgemein, allumfassend; general administration: Hauptverwaltung *(f)*; general authority/power: Generalvollmacht *(f)*; General Certificate of Education: Reifezeugnis *(n)*; general company meeting: Hauptversammlung *(f)*; general customs *(Pl)*: Gewohnheitsrecht *(n)*; general education: (gute) Allgemeinbildung *(f)*; general knowledge: Allgemeinbildung *(f)*; general obligation (of a tariff agreement): Allgemeinverbindlichkeit *(f)* eines Tarifvertrages; general stockholders' meeting: Aktionärsversammlung *(f)*, Hauptversammlung *(f)*; general strike: Generalstreik *(m)*.

German Federal Armed Forces — Bundeswehr *(f)*.

get *(v)* **together** — sich einigen, zusammenfinden.

getup ⟨AE⟩ — Initiative *(f)*.

gift — Begabung *(f)*.

gifted *(adj)* — begabt.

giri apprentice — Lehrmädchen *(n)*, weibliche Auszubildende *(f)*.

gliding time — Gleitzeit *(f)*.

global amount — Pauschale *(f)*.

go-slow ⟨BE⟩ — planmäßiges Langsamarbeiten *(n)*, Bummelstreik *(m)*.

good conduct certificate — Führungszeugnis *(n)*.

good faith — Treu und Glauben ⟨Ausdr.⟩.

governing board (of directors) — Hauptvorstand (m).

government service — Staatsdienst (m).

grade — Einstufungsgruppe (f), Grad (m).

grading of wages — Lohnstaffelung (f).

graduate education — Akademikerausbildung (f).

grammar school ⟨BE⟩ — Gymnasium (n); grammar-school education: Gymnasialausbildung (f); grammar-school student: Gymnasiast(in) (m ⟨f⟩).

grant — Stipendium (n), Studienbeihilfe (f), (staatlicher) Zuschuß (m).

graphology — Graphologie (f).

gratification — Belohnung (f), Honorar (n).

gratuity — Belohnung (f), Vergütung (f), Tantieme (f).

grievance — Beschwerde (f), Klage (f), Beschwerdefall (m); grievance committee: Beschwerdestelle (f); grievance procedure: Beschwerdeverfahren (n).

gross hourly wages (Pl) — Bruttostundenverdienst (m).

gross wage/earnings (Pl) — Bruttolohn (m).

ground for giving notice — Kündigungsgrund (m).

grounds (Pl) **for discharge** — Entlassungsgrund (m).

group — Gruppe (f); group dynamics (Pl): Gruppendynamik (f); group incentive: Gruppenakkord (m), Gruppenprämie (f); group leader: Kolonnenführer(in) (m ⟨f⟩); group output: Gruppenleistung (f); group piece rate: Gruppenakkordlohn (m); group supervisor: Gruppenleiter(in) (m ⟨f⟩); group-term life insurance: Gruppenlebensversicherung (f).

groupage rate — Gruppentarif (m).

guarantee — Bürgschaft (f), Haftung (f).

guard rail — Schutzgeländer (n).

guardianship — vormundschaftliche Aufsicht (f).

guide (v) — führen.

H

half-day/-time job — Halbtagsarbeit (f), Halbtagsbeschäftigung (f).

half-time (adj) — halbtags, halbtägig.

half-timer — Halbtagskraft (f).

handbook — Handbuch (n).

handicap — Erschwernis (n).

handicapped (adj) — (körper-)behindert.

handicraft — Handfertigkeit (f).

handicraftsman — Handwerker (m).

handiwork — Handarbeit (f).

handwork — Handarbeit (f) ⟨Arbeitsausführung⟩.

handwriting — Handschrift (f).

handwritten (adj) — handschriftlich.

hard hat — Schutzhelm (m).

hard work — Schwerarbeit (f).

harmful (adj) — gesundheitsschädlich, gesundheitsschädigend.

hazard bonus — Gefahrenzulage (f).

head — Chef(in) *(m ⟨f⟩)*, Leiter(in) *(m ⟨f⟩)*.

head clerc — Bürovorsteher(in) *(m ⟨f⟩)*.

headcount — Personalstärke *(f)*.

headquarters — Hauptverwaltung *(f)*.

health — Gesundheit *(f)*; health certificate: Gesundheitsattest *(n)*, Gesundheitsnachweis *(m)*; health hazards *(Pl)*: Gesundheitsschäden *(m, Pl)*; health insurance: Krankenversicherung *(f)*; health insurance company/scheme/plan: Krankenkasse *(f)*; health insurance premium: Krankenversicherungsbeitrag *(m)*; health service: Gesundheitsdienst *(m)*.

heat treat operation — Warmbetrieb *(m)*.

help(er) — Aushilfe *(f)*, Hilfskraft *(f)*.

high industrial activity — Hochkonjunktur *(f)*.

high school ⟨AE⟩ — Gymnasium *(n)*.

high-school graduation ⟨AE⟩ — Abitur *(n)*.

hire *(v)* — anwerben, einstellen.

hiring — Einstellung *(f)* von Personal.

hold — Haft *(f)*.

holiday ⟨BE⟩ — Ferien *(Pl)*, Urlaub *(m)*, Feiertag *(m)*, Erholung *(f)*; collectively agreed holidays *(Pl)*: Tarifurlaub *(m)*; holiday post: Ferienbeschäftigung *(f)*; holiday premium: Feiertagszuschlag *(m)*; holiday schedule: Ferienordnung *(f)*; holiday season: Ferienzeit *(f)*; holiday work: Ferienarbeit . *(f)*; holiday replacement: Urlaubsvertretung *(f)*.

home address — Heimatanschrift *(f)*.

home leave — Heimaturlaub *(m)*.

homeworker — Heimarbeiter(in) *(m ⟨f⟩)*.

honorarium — Honorar *(n)*.

honorary *(adj)* — ehrenamtlich; honorary post/function/office: Ehrenamt *(n)*.

hourly paid employee — Lohnempfänger(in) *(m ⟨f⟩)*.

hourly wage (rate) — Stundenlohn *(m)*.

hours worked per week — Wochenarbeitszeit *(f)*.

household help — Haushaltshilfe *(f)*.

housewife — Hausfrau *(f)*.

housing loan — Wohnungsbaudarlehn *(n)*.

human engineering ⟨AE⟩ — Arbeitsplatzgestaltung *(f)*.

I

idle *(adj)* — untätig, träge, ohne Beschäftigung; make *(v)* idle: (Arbeitskräfte) freisetzen.

illegal *(adj)* — gesetzwidrig, ungesetzlich.

illicit work — Schwarzarbeit *(f)*.

illitracy — Bildungsmangel *(m)*.

immigrant worker — Gastarbeiter *(m)*, Fremdarbeiter *(m)*.

imperdiment — Erschwernis *(f)*.

imprisonment — Haft *(f)*.

improvement of one's knowledge/training — Fortbildung *(f)*.

in-hospital benefit — Krankenhausbeihilfe *(f)*.

in-plant *(adj)* ⟨AE⟩ — innerbetrieblich.

inability — Unvermögen *(n)*; inability to work: Arbeitsunfähigkeit *(f)*.

inactive period — Ausfallzeit *(f)* ⟨Versicherung⟩.

incalculable *(adj)* — unzuverlässig.

incapable *(adj)* — unfähig; incapable of work: arbeitsunfähig.

incapacitation — Entmündigung *(f)*.

incapacity for employment — Erwerbsunfähigkeit *(f)*; incapacity from working/to work/for work: Arbeitsunfähigkeit *(f)*.

incentive — Leistungsanreiz *(m)*.

incentive *(adj)* — leistungssteigernd, anspornend; incentive bonus system: Prämiensystem *(n)*; incentive pay/wages *(Pl)*: Leistungslohn *(m)*.

incidental expenses *(Pl)* — Spesen *(Pl)*.

income — Einkommen *(n)*, Bezüge *(Pl)*, Verdienst *(m)*; income tax relief ⟨BE⟩: Freibetrag *(m)* bei der Einkommensteuer.

increase — Steigerung *(f)*, Zuwachs *(m)*; increase in efficiency/performance: Leistungssteigerung *(f)*; increase in production: Produktionsanstieg *(m)*; increase in productivity: Produktivitätszuwachs *(m)*; increase in scale wages/salaries: Tariferhöhung *(f)*; increase of standard wage: Tariflohnerhöhung *(f)*.

increased performance/efficiency — Mehrleistung *(f)*.

incumbent — Stelleninhaber(in) *(m ⟨f⟩)*.

indemnification — Entschädigung *(f)*, Abfindung *(f)*.

indemnify *(v)* — jmd. abfinden.

indemnity — Abgeltungsbetrag *(m)*, Abfindung *(f)*, Schadenersatz *(m)*.

indenture — Lehrvertrag *(m)*.

indirect cost — Betriebsgemeinkosten *(Pl)*.

individual workplace — Einzelarbeitsplatz *(m)*.

indoor work — Heimarbeit *(f)*.

induction order ⟨AE⟩ — Einberufungsbefehl *(m)* ⟨mil.⟩.

industrial *(adj)* — gewerblich, industriell; industrial accident/injury: Betriebsunfall *(m)*; industrial action: Arbeitskampf *(m)*; industrial activity: Gewerbetätigkeit *(f)*; industrial code: Gewerbeordnung *(f)*; industrial conflict: Arbeitskonflikt *(m)*; industrial consultant: Betriebsberater(in) *(m ⟨f⟩)*; industrial disease: Berufskrankheit *(f)*; industrial engineer: Betriebsingenieur(in) *(m ⟨f⟩)*; industrial engineering: Arbeitsvorbereitung *(f)*; industrial estate/area/park ⟨AE⟩: Industriegelände *(n)*; industrial experience: Industrieerfahrung *(f)*; industrial front ⟨BE⟩: Streikfront *(f)*; industrial hygiene: Arbeitshygiene *(f)*; industrial inspection office/board: Gewerbeaufsichtsamt *(n)*, Gewerbeaufsichtsbehörde *(f)*; industrial insurance: Gewerbeunfallversicherung *(f)*; industrial law ⟨BE⟩: Arbeitsrecht *(n)*, Gewerberecht *(n)*; industrial medicine: Arbeitsmedizin *(f)*; industrial peace: Arbeitsfrieden *(m)*; industrial psychology: Arbeitspsychologie *(f)*; industrial safety: Arbeitsschutz *(m)*; industrial school: Berufsschule *(f)*; industrial trainee: Praktikant(in) *(m ⟨f⟩)*; industrial tribunal ⟨BE⟩: Arbeitsgericht *(n)*; industrial union: Industriegewerkschaft *(f)*; industrial worker/labo(u)rer: Fabrikarbeiter(in) *(m ⟨f⟩)*, Industriearbeiter(in) *(m ⟨f⟩)*.

industry — Produktionszweig *(m)*.

inefficiency — Leistungsverlust *(m)*.

initial *(adj)* — anfänglich, ursprünglich; initial payment: Anzahlung *(f)*, Teilzahlung *(f)*; initial salary: Anfangsgehalt *(n)*; initial vote: Urabstimmung *(f)*.

initiative — Initiative *(f)*.

injunction — einstweilige Verfügung *(f)*.

injurious *(adj)* **to health** — gesundheitsgefährdend.

injury investigation report — Unfallbericht *(m)*.

injury to one's health — Gesundheitsschaden *(m)*.

insanitary *(adj)* — gesundheitsschädlich.

insert *(v)* — Inserat aufgeben, inserieren.

insertion — Inserat *(n)*.

insolvency — Konkurs *(m)*.

inspection — Aufsicht *(f)*.

inspector general — Oberinspektor *(m)*.

instalment (payment) — Teilzahlung *(f)*.

instruct *(v)* — jmd. einarbeiten, einweisen, anlernen, anweisen.

instruction — Anweisung *(f)*, Einweisung *(f)*, Ausbildung *(f)* auf einem Gebiet; give *(v)* initial instruction: jmd. anlernen.

insurance liability limit — Versicherungspflichtgrenze *(f)*.

intercity (wage) differential — Ortsklassenausgleich *(m)*.

intercompany *(adj)* — innerbetrieblich, firmenintern.

interdiction — Entmündigung *(f)*.

interest — Interesse *(n)*, Anteil *(m)*, Anrecht *(n)*, Beteiligung *(f)*.

interim aid — Überbrückungsbeihilfe *(f)*.

intermediate examination — Zwischenprüfung *(f)*.

interoffice slip — Laufzettel *(m)*.

invalidating cause — Anfechtungsgrund *(m)*.

invalidity — Invalidität *(f)*, Gebrechlichkeit *(f)*.

irrevocable *(adj)* — unkündbar, unwiderruflich.

J

jib *(v)* ⟨colloq.⟩ — streiken.

job — Tätigkeit *(f)*, Beschäftigung *(f)*, Beruf *(m)*, Arbeit *(f)*, Amt *(n)*, Stelle *(f)*, Position *(f)*; job analysis: Arbeitsanalyse *(f)*; job applicant: Stellenbewerber(in) *(m* ⟨f⟩*)*; job content: Arbeitsinhalt *(m)*; job description: Arbeitsplatzbeschreibung *(f)*, Tätigkeitsbeschreibung *(f)*; job design: Arbeitsplatzgestaltung *(f)* ⟨äußere⟩; job engineering: Arbeitsplatzgestaltung *(f)* ⟨inhaltliche⟩; job enlargement: Aufgabenerweiterung *(f)*; job enrichment: Aufgabenanreicherung *(f)*; job evaluation: Arbeitsbewertung *(f)*; job leasing: Leiharbeit *(f)*; job market: Arbeitsstellenmarkt *(m)*; job nomenclature: Berufsbezeichnung *(f)*; job opportunity/opening: Stellenangebot *(n)*, offene Stelle *(f)*; job order: Arbeitsauftrag *(m)*; job prospects *(Pl)*: Berufsaussichten *(Pl)*; job report: Arbeitsbericht *(m)*; job satisfaction: Arbeitszufriedenheit *(f)*; job security: Arbeitsplatzsicherheit *(f)*; job seeker: Arbeitssuchender *(m)*; job specification ⟨AE⟩: Arbeitsplatzbeschreibung *(f)*; job ticket: Akkordzettel *(m)*; job title ⟨AE⟩: Berufsbezeichnung *(f)*; job work: Stückakkord *(m)*; job worker: Akkordarbeiter *(m)*.

jobbing hand — Akkordarbeiter *(m)*.

jobholder — Stelleninhaber(in) *(m* ⟨f⟩*)*.

jobless *(adj)* — arbeitslos, ohne Beschäftigung.

join *(v)* **in the work** — mitarbeiten.

joint signature — Gesamtprokura *(f)*.

journeyman — Gehilfe *(m)*, Geselle *(m)*,

Handwerksbursche *(m)*; journeyman's (final) examination: Gesellenprüfung *(f)*.

journeywoman — Gesellin *(f)*.

jubilarian — Jubilar(in) *(m ⟨f⟩)*.

jubilee — Jubiläum *(n)*.

juridical *(adj)* — gerichtlich.

jurisdiction — Rechtsprechung *(f)*; jurisdiction over industrial matters: Arbeitsgerichtsverfahren *(n)*.

K

knocking-off time *⟨colloq.⟩* — Arbeitsschluß *(m)*.

knowledge — Bildung *(f, Pl)*.

L

labor *⟨AE⟩*, **labour** *⟨BE⟩* — Arbeit *(f)*; labo(u)r (market) situation: Beschäftigungslage *(f)*, Arbeitsmarktlage *(f)*; labo(u)r allocation: Arbeitszuweisung *(f)*, Arbeitseinsatz *(m)*; labo(u)r conflict: Arbeitskonflikt *(m)*; labo(u)r contract: Arbeitsvertrag *(m)*; labo(u)r cost: Arbeitskosten *(Pl)*; labo(u)r costs *(Pl)*: Arbeitskosten *(Pl)*, Lohnkosten *(Pl)*; labo(u)r court: Arbeitsgericht *(n)*; Labo(u)r Court Act: Arbeitsgerichtsgesetz *(n)*; labo(u)r court judge: Arbeitsrichter(in) *(m ⟨f⟩)*; labo(u)r director: Arbeitsdirektor *(m)*; labo(u)r dispute: Arbeitskampf *(m)*; labo(u)r intensive *(adj)*: arbeitsintensiv; labo(u)r jurisdiction: Arbeitsrechtsprechung *(f)*; labo(u)r legislation: Arbeitsgesetzgebung *(f)*; labo(u)r market: Arbeitsmarkt *(m)*; labo(u)r market area: Arbeitskräfte-Einzugsgebiet *(n)*; labo(u)r movement: Arbeiterbewegung *(f)*; labo(u)r piracy: Abwerbung *(f)* von Arbeitskräften; labo(u)r saving: Arbeitsersparnis *(f)*; labo(u)r shortage: Arbeitskräftemangel *(m)*; labo(u)r-management relations: Arbeitnehmer-Arbeitgeber-Beziehungen *(f, Pl)*; labo(u)rer: unge-

lernte(r)) Arbeiter(in) *(m ⟨f⟩)*; Labor Department *⟨AE⟩*: Arbeitsministerium *(n)*; labor law *⟨AE⟩*: Arbeitsrecht *(n)*; labor office *⟨AE⟩*: Arbeitsamt *(n)*; labor union *⟨AE⟩*: Gewerkschaft *(f)*; labour exchange *⟨BE⟩*: Arbeitsamt *(n)*.

lady housekeeper — Haushälterin *(f)*.

lady typist — Stenotypistin *(f)*.

land labo(u)r court — Landesarbeitsgericht *(n)*.

lapse from one's duty — Pflichtverletzung *(f)*.

large establishment — Großbetrieb *(m)*.

large-scale enterprise — Großbetrieb *(m)*.

law — Gesetz *(n)*; according/by law: gesetzlich; law breaking: Gesetzesverstoß *(m)*; law of practice/procedure: Prozeßrecht *(n)*; lawful *(adj)*: gesetzlich zulässig, dem Gesetz entsprechend; lawsuit: Rechtsstreit *(m)*, Prozeß *(m)*, Klage *(f)*.

lay judge — Laienrichter(in) *(m ⟨f⟩)* Beisitzer(in) *(m ⟨f⟩)* bei Gericht.

layoff *⟨AE⟩* — vorübergehende Entlas-

sung *(f)*; layoff benefit: Entlassungsentschädigung *(f)*.

lazy *(adj)* — faul.

lead *(v)* — führen.

leadership potential — Führungspotential *(n)*.

leadership quality — Führungseigenschaft *(f)*.

learn *(v)* — lernen.

learner — Anlernling *(m)*; learner's wage
rate: Anlernlohn *(m)*.

learning — Bildung *(f)*.

lease contract — Mietvertrag *(m)*.

leave — Abschied *(m)*, Erlaubnis *(f)*; go
(v) on leave: auf/in Urlaub gehen; give
(v) s.o. leave: jmd. beurlauben; leave of
absence: Urlaub *(m)*; leave pay: Urlaubsgeld *(n)*; leave schedule: Urlaubsplan *(m)*.

leaving certificate — Abgangszeugnis
(n), Reifezeugnis *(n)*.

leaving examination — Reifeprüfung
(f).

legal *(adj)* — gesetzlich, juristisch; legal
action: Klage *(f)*; legal capacity: Geschäftsfähigkeit *(f)*; having legal capacity: geschäftsfähig sein; legal
knowledge: Rechtskenntnisse *(f, Pl)*;
legal mandate: Prozeßvollmacht *(f)*;
legal matters: Prozeßsache *(f)*; legally
compentent/responsible *(adj)*: geschäftsfähig; legally liable *(adj)*: gesetzlich haftbar.

legislation — Gesetzgebung *(f)*.

legitimate *(adj)* — mit berechtigtem Anspruch auf, ehelich ⟨Kind⟩, gesetzlich.

leisure — Freizeit *(f)*; leisure service:
Freizeitgestaltungsprogramm *(n)*;
leisure time: Feierabend *(m)*.

length of continous employment —
Dauer *(f)* der Betriebszugehörigkeit.

letter of confirmation — Bestätigungsschreiben *(n)*.

letters *(Pl)* **of commendation** — Empfehlungsbrief *(m)*.

level of production/output — Produktionsstand *(m)*.

level of unemployment — Arbeitslosen-
stand *(m)*.

levy — Pfändung *(f)*.

liability — Verpflichtung *(f)*, Pflicht *(f)*,
Haftung *(f)*; liability insurance: Haftpflichtversicherung *(f)*; liability to contribute: Beitragspflicht *(f)*; liability to insure: Versicherungspflicht *(f)*; liability
to notice: Kündbarkeit *(f)*.

liable *(adj)* — haftbar, verantwortlich; legally liable gesetzlich haftbar; liable
to military service: wehrpflichtig; liable
for payment/services: leistungspflichtig.

life insurance/assurance ⟨BE⟩ — Lebensversicherung *(f)*.

limit *(v)* s.o. as to time — befristen.

limitation (of time) — Verjährung *(f)*.

line of conduct — Lebenswandel *(m)*.

list of employe(e)s — Personalliste *(f)*.

litigious person — Querulant(in) *(m* ⟨f⟩*)*.

livelihood — Lebensunterhalt *(m)*.

living costs *(Pl)* — Lebenshaltungskosten *(Pl)*.

loaf *(v)* — faulenzen, herumlungern, sich
herumtreiben; be on the loaf: faulenzen.

loafer — Faulenzer *(m)*.

lockout — Aussperrung *(f)*.

locksmith — Schlosser(in) *(m* ⟨f⟩*)*.

lodgement — Mietwohnung *(f)*.

lodging allowance/money — Wohngeldzuschuß *(m)*, Mietzulage *(f)*.

lodgings *(Pl)* — Mietwohnung *(f)*.

longshoreman ⟨*AE*⟩ — Hafenarbeiter *(m)*.

loss — Verlust *(m)*, Ausfall *(m)*; loss of remuneration: Verdienstausfall *(m)*; loss of wages/pay/earnings: Lohnausfall *(m)*; loss of working hours/time: Arbeitsausfall *(m)*.

lump-sum — Pauschale *(f)*; lump-sum compensation: Pauschalabfindung *(f)*; lump-sum mileage allowance: Kilometergeldpauschale *(f)*; lump-sum payment: Pauschalzahlung *(f)*; lump-sum settlement: Pauschalentschädigung *(f)*, Pauschalabgeltung *(f)*.

lunch break — Mittagspause *(f)*.

lunchroom ⟨*AE*⟩ — Kantine *(f)*.

M

machine fitter — Maschinenschlosser(in) *(m ⟨f⟩)*.

machinist — Maschinenarbeiter(in) *(m ⟨f⟩)*.

maid (servant) ⟨*AE*⟩ — Hausangestellte *(f)*.

main *(adj)* — hauptsächlich; main department: Hauptabteilung *(f)*; main profession: Hauptberuf *(m)*, Haupterwerbszweig *(m)*; main study: Hauptstudium *(n)*; main subject: Hauptfach *(n)* ⟨*Schule*⟩.

maintenance — Unterhalt *(m)*, Instandhaltung *(f)*; maintenance employe(e)s *(Pl)* — Instandhaltungspersonal *(n)*.

major *(adj)* — volljährig.

major ⟨*AE*⟩ — Hauptfach *(n)*.

majority vote — Mehrheitswahl *(f)*.

make-up day — Vor-/Nachholtag *(m)*.

make-up pay — Akkordzuschlag *(m)*.

make-up work — Vor-/Nachholarbeit *(f)*.

malinger *(v)* — krankfeiern.

manage *(v)* — leiten, führen.

management — Betriebsleitung *(f)*; management board: Vorstand *(m)*; management consultant: Unternehmensberater *(m)*; management skills *(Pl)*: Führungsqualitäten *(f, Pl)*; management style: Führungsstil *(m)*; management trainees *(Pl)*: Führungsnachwuchs *(m)*.

manager — Leiter *(m)*, Führungskraft *(f)*.

managerial *(adj)* — Leitungs-/Führungs-; managerial authority: Führungsbefugnis *(f)*; managerial employe(e): leitende(r) Angestellte(r) *(m ⟨f⟩)*; managerial level: Führungsebene *(f)*; managerial quality: Führungseigenschaft *(f)*; managerial techniques *(Pl)*: Führungsmethode *(f)*.

managing *(adj)* — geschäftsführend.

manhour — Arbeitsstunde *(f)*, ⟨*Produktionseinheit*⟩.

manhours *(Pl)* — aufgewandte Zeit *(f)*, Arbeitsleistung *(f)*.

manning — personelle Ausstattung *(f)*, Besetzung *(f)*; manning table: Stellenbesetzungsplan *(m)*.

manpower — Arbeitskräfte *(f, Pl)*; manpower planning: quantitative Personalplanung *(f)*; manpower requirement: Arbeitskräftebedarf *(m)*; manpower shortage: Personalmangel *(m)*.

manual — Handbuch *(n)*.

manual *(adj)* — mit der Hand arbeitend, eigenhändig; manual skill: Handfertigkeit *(f)*; manual worker: Handarbeiter *(m)*, gewerblicher Arbeitnehmer *(m)*.

manufacture — Produktion *(m)*, Herstellung *(f)*.

manufacture *(v)* — herstellen, produzieren.

manufacturer's public liability — Betriebshaftpflicht *(f)*.

manufacturing industry — produzierendes Gewerbe *(n)*.

manufacturing plant — Produktionsbetrieb *(m)*, Produktionsstätte *(f)*.

marital *(adj)* — ehelich; marital partner: Ehegatte *(m)*, Ehegattin *(f)*, Ehepartner(in) *(m ⟨f⟩)*.

market prospects *(Pl)* — Konjunktur *(f)*.

marriage — Heirat *(f)*, Hochzeit *(f)*.

marriage allowance — Heiratsbeihilfe *(f)*; marriage certificate: Heiratsurkunde *(f)*; marriage grant: Ehestandsbeihilfe *(f)*; marriage loan: Ehestandsdarlehen *(n)*.

mass — Masse *(f)*, Menge *(f)*; mass release/dismissals *(Pl)* — Massenentlassung *(f)*; mass strike: Generalstreik *(m)*; mass unemployment: Massenarbeitslosigkeit *(f)*.

master (of trade) — Handwerksmeister *(m)*; master craftsman's certificate: Meisterbrief *(m)*.

master mechanic — Vorarbeiter *(m)*.

material *(adj)* — körperlich.

maternity — Mutterschaft *(f)*; maternity benefit: Geburtenbeihilfe *(f)*; maternity protection: Mutterschutz *(m)*; Maternity Protection Act: Mutterschutzgesetz *(n)*.

matrimonial *(adj)* — ehelich.

matter for negotiation — Verhandlungsgegenstand *(m)*.

maximum *(adj)* — höchst, größt; maximum age: Höchstalter *(n)*; maximum time of work: Höchstarbeitszeit *(f)*; maximum wage: Spitzenlohn *(m)*, Höchstlohn *(m)*; maximum working time/hours: Höchstarbeitszeit *(f)*.

meal break — Essenspause *(f)*.

meal ticket/voucher — Essenmarke *(f)*, Essenbon *(m)*.

means *(Pl)* **of production** — Produktionsmittel *(n, Pl)*.

mechanic — Mechaniker(in) *(m ⟨f⟩)*.

mechanical engineer — Maschinenbauingenieur *(m)*.

mediation committee — Schlichtungsausschuß *(m)*, Schlichtungsstelle *(f)*, Vermittlungsausschuß *(m)*.

mediator — Schlichter *(m)*, Vermittler *(m)*.

medical *(adj)* — ärztlich; medical care: ärztliche Versorgung *(f)*; medical certificate: ärztliches Zeugnis *(n)*, Attest *(n)*; medical examination: ärztliche Untersuchung *(f)*; medical examiner: Vertrauensarzt *(m)*, Vertrauensärztin *(f)*.

member of a (trade/labour) union — Gewerkschaft(l)er(in) *(m ⟨f⟩)*.

mentally handicapped/retarded *(adj)* — geistig behindert.

mercantile *(adj)* — kaufmännisch.

merchant's clerk — Handlungsgehilfe *(m)*, Handlungsgehilfin *(f)*.

merit — Verdienst *(n)*; according to merit: leistungsbedingt; merit bonus: Leistungsprämie *(f)*, Leistungszulage *(f)*; merit increase: leistungsbezogene Lohn-/Gehaltserhöhung *(f)*; merit rating: Leistungsbewertung *(f)*.

method of work/operation — Arbeitsmethode *(f)*.

method-time-measurement ("MTM") — Elementarzeitbestimmungssystem *(n)*.

mileage allowance — Kilometergeld *(n)*.

mine safety — Grubensicherheit *(f)*.

miner — Grubenarbeiter *(m)*, Bergmann *(m)*; miner's insurance: Knappschaft *(f)*; miner's provident/benefit fund: Knappschaftskasse *(f)*.

Ministry of Labour ⟨*BE*⟩ — Arbeitsministerium *(n)*.

minor occupation — Nebenberuf *(m)*.

money transfer — Geldüberweisung *(f)*.

moneyed *(adj)* — kaufkräftig ⟨*Käufer*⟩.

moral strength — Charakterfestigkeit *(f)*.

morning shift — Frühschicht *(f)*.

motherhood — Mutterschaft *(f)*.

move ⟨*AE*⟩ — Umzug *(m)*.

move *(v)* — jmd. versetzen/umsetzen, umziehen.

moving line — Fließband *(n)*; (moving) line manning: (Fließ-)Bandbesetzung *(f)*; (moving) line speed: (Fließ-)Bandgeschwindigkeit *(f)*.

muster — Musterung *(f)* ⟨*mil*⟩.

mutual *(adj)* — gegenseitig.

N

national assistance ⟨*BE*⟩ — Sozialhilfe *(f)*.

national insurance ⟨*BE*⟩ — Sozialversicherung *(f)*; national insurance contribution ⟨*BE*⟩: Sozialversicherungsbeitrag *(m)*.

national service ⟨*BE*⟩ — Militärdienst *(m)*.

native place — Heimatort *(m)*, Geburtsort *(m)*.

nature — Charakter *(m)*.

need — Mangel *(m)*, Bedarf *(m)*, Knappheit *(f)*.

needy *(adj)* — hilfsbedürftig.

negligence — Verschulden *(n)*.

negotiate *(v)* — verhandeln, aushandeln.

negotiation (on, about, over) — Verhandlung *(f)* (über); negotiation outcome: Verhandlungsergebnis *(n)*.

night school — Abendkursus *(m)*.

night shift — Nachtschicht *(f)*; night shift premium: Nachtschichtzulage *(f)*.

nightwork — Nachtarbeit *(f)*; nightwork premium: Nachtarbeitszuschlag *(m)*.

nominal manhours *(Pl)* — Sollarbeitsstunden *(f, Pl)*.

non occupational *(adj)* — berufsfremd.

nonprofit-making *(adj)* — gemeinnützig.

normal performance — Normalleistung *(f)*.

notice — Aushang *(m)*, Nachricht *(f)*.

notice (of termination) — Kündigung *(f)*; subject to notice: kündbar; written notice: Kündigungsschreiben *(n)*; give *(v)* notice to s.o. (to terminate work): jmd. kündigen; give *(v)* s.o. notice (of termination): jmd. kündigen; notice board: Aushangbrett *(n)*; notice of termination of agreed wages/salaries: Tarifkündigung *(f)*; notice of termination of scale of rates/charges: Tarifkündigung *(f)*; notice period: Kündigungsfrist *(f)*; notice to quit: Aufkündigung *(f)* der Dienste.

notifiable *(adj)* — anzeigepflichtig ⟨*Krankheit*⟩.

notification of change (of the terms of employment) — Änderungskündigung *(f)*.

noxious *(adj)* — gesundheitsgefährdend, gesundheitsschädlich.

number of personnel — Personalstand *(m)*, Beschäftigungszahl *(f)*.

O

object of negotiation — Verhandlungsgegenstand *(m)*.

obligation — Pflicht *(f)*, Verpflichtung *(f)*; obligation for loyalty/faith — Treuepflicht *(f)*, ⟨*Arbeitnehmer*⟩; obligation to insure: Versicherungspflicht *(f)*; obligation to pay social insurance contributions: Sozialversicherungspflicht *(f)*.

obtaining of a doctorate — Promotion *(f)*.

occasional work — Gelegenheitsarbeit *(f)*.

occupation — Beschäftigung *(f)*, Beruf *(m)*, Tätigkeit *(f)*; as a secondary occupation: nebenberuflich; as a regular occupation: hauptberuflich.

occupational *(adj)* — beruflich; occupational accident: Berufsunfall *(m)*; occupational decision: Berufswahl *(f)*; occupational disease: Berufskrankheit *(f)*; occupational education: Berufsbildung *(f)*; occupational group: Berufsgruppe *(f)*; occupational hazard: Berufsrisiko *(n)*; occupational illness: Berufskrankheit *(f)*; occupational injury: Berufsunfall *(m)*; occupational name: Berufsbezeichnung *(f)*; occupational risk: Berufsrisiko *(n)*; occupational safety: Arbeitssicherheit *(f)*; occupational training: Fachausbildung *(f)*; occupational wage: Facharbeiterlohn *(m)*.

occupy *(v)* — jmd. beschäftigen.

off-setting provision — Anrechnungsklausel *(f)*.

offer — Angebot *(n)*.

office — Büro *(n)*, Amt *(n)*, Aufgabe *(f)*, Dienst *(m)*; accede *(v)*/come *(v)* into/enter up *(v)*/take *(v)* an office: Amt *(n)* antreten; relinquish *(v)*/vacate *(v)* an office: Amt *(n)* aufgeben; hold *(v)*/keep *(v)*/bear *(v)* an office: Amt *(n)* innehaben; office boy: Bürogehilfe *(m)*/Bürogehilfin *(f)*; office clerc: Büroangestellte(r) *(f ⟨m⟩)*; office day: Arbeitstag *(m)*; office equipment: Büroeinrichtung *(f)*; office hours *(Pl)*: Sprechstunde *(f)*, Bürozeit *(f)*; office keeper: Bürovorsteher(in) *(m ⟨f⟩)*.

officer of the reserve — Reserveoffizier *(m)*.

official *(adj)* — dienstlich; official call: Dienstgespräch *(n)*; official duty: Dienstpflicht *(f)*; official in charge: Sachbearbeiter(in) *(m ⟨f⟩)*; official trip: Dienstreise *(f)*.

old-age and survivors' insurance — Alters- und Hinterbliebenenversorgung *(f)*.

old-age pension — Altersrente *(f)*, Pension *(f)*, Ruhegehalt *(n)*; old-age pension fund: Altersversorgungskasse *(f)*.

old-age pensioner — Rentner(in) *(m ⟨f⟩)* Pensionär(in) *(m ⟨f⟩)*.

once-for-all-payment — Einmalzahlung *(f)*.

operating *(adj)* — betrieblich, in Betrieb befindlich; operating trouble: Betriebsausfall *(m)*.

operation — Arbeitsvorgang *(m)*, Verfahren *(n)*, Betrieb *(m)*.

operational *(adj)* — betriebsbedingt, betrieblich, funktionsbedingt; operational hazard: Betriebsgefahr *(f)*; operational method: Arbeitsmethode *(f)*; operational risk: Betriebsgefahr *(f)*.

operations manager — Betriebsleiter *(m)*.

operations scheduling — Arbeitsvorbereitung *(f)*.

operative — Mechaniker(in) *(m ⟨f⟩)*.

operative *(adj)* — betrieblich; operative procedure: Betriebsablauf *(m)*.

operator — Arbeiter(in) *(m ⟨f⟩) ⟨an Maschine⟩*, Telefonist(in) *(m ⟨f⟩)*, Filmvorführer(in) *(m ⟨f⟩)*.

opinion poll/research — Meinungsbefragung *(f)*.

opponent of a strike — Streikgegner *(m)*.

opposing party — Prozeßgegner(in) *(m ⟨f⟩)*.

order — Anordnung *(f)*, Anweisung *(f)*, Verfügung *(f)*.

organisation chart — Organisationsplan *(m)*.

organizing chart — Geschäftsverteilungsplan *(m)*.

original income — Anfangsbezüge *(Pl)*.

out of job/employ/work — beschäftigungslos, arbeitslos, erwerbslos.

out of order *(adj)* — kaputt, außer Betrieb.

outlays *(Pl)* — Spesen *(Pl)*, Auslagen *(f, Pl)*.

output — Produktionsmenge *(f)*, Arbeit *(f)*, Leistung *(f)*, Erzeugnis *(n)*; output figure: Produktionsziffer *(f)*; output per (man-)shift: Schichtleistung *(f)*; output rate: Produktionsziffer *(f)*; output restriction: Produktionsbeschränkung *(f)*.

outwork — Heimarbeit *(f)*.

outworker — Heimarbeiter(in) *(m ⟨f⟩)*.

overall *(adj)* — gesamt; overall compensation: Pauschalabfindung *(f)*; overall efficiency: Gesamtleistung *(f)*; overall employment: Gesamtheit *(f)* der Beschäftigten.

overcharge — Mehrbelastung *(f)*.

overhead — (Betriebs-)Gemeinkosten *(Pl)*; overhead rate: Gemeinkostenanteil *(m)*.

overload — Über(be)lastung *(f)*.

overseer — Schichtmeister *(m)*.

overstrain o.s. *(v)* — sich überarbeiten.

overtime — Überstunden *(f, Pl)*, Mehrarbeit *(f)*; overtime ban: Mehrarbeitsstop *(m)*, Überstundenverbot *(n)*; overtime hour: Überstunde *(f)*; overtime pay(ment): Mehrarbeitsvergütung *(f)*, Überstundenbezahlung *(f)*; overtime premium/bonus: Überstundenzuschlag *(m)*, Mehrarbeitszuschlag *(m)*; overtime work: Mehrarbeit *(f)*, Mehrarbeitsleistung *(f)*.

overwork — Arbeitsüberlastung *(f)*.

P

package claim — Gesamtforderung *(f)*, Forderungspaket *(n)*.

paid labo(u)r — Lohnarbeit *(f)*.

pains *(Pl)* — Mühe *(f)*, Arbeit *(f)*.

parity — Parität *(f)*; parity of wages: Lohnparität *(f)*.

particulars *(Pl)* — Personalangaben *(f, Pl)*, Daten *(n, Pl)*.

part-time *(adj)* — halbtags, halbtätig; part-time job: Halbtagsstelle *(f)*; part-time vocational school: Berufsschule *(f)*; part-time work: Teilzeitarbeit *(f)*.

part-timer — Halbtags-/Teilzeitkraft *(f)*.

part(ial) payment — Teilzahlung *(f)*.

participate *(v)* **in the management** — mitbestimmen ⟨im Betrieb⟩.

participation — Mitwirkung *(f)*.

party to a (collective) agreement — Tarifpartner *(m)*, Tarifvertragspartei *(f)*.

pause — Arbeitspause *(f)*.

pay *(v)* — bezahlen, vergüten, besolden; pay s.o. *(v)* compensation: jmd. abfinden; pay off *(v)*: jmd. abfinden.

pay — Bezahlung *(f)*, Entlohnung *(f)*, Arbeitsentgelt *(n)*, Arbeitslohn *(m)*; pay agreement: Lohnabkommen *(n)*; pay bill: Lohn-/Gehaltsliste *(f)*; pay cut: Entgeltkürzung *(f)*, Lohnsenkung *(f)*; pay dispute: Lohnauseinandersetzung *(f)*; pay fixing: Lohnfestsetzung *(f)*; Pay for Public Holidays Act ⟨Act respecting the payment of wages for public holidays⟩: Feiertagslohnzahlungsgesetz *(n)*; pay for shift work: Schichtlohn *(m)*; pay increase: Lohnerhöhung *(f)*; pay increment: Lohnzuwachs *(m)*; pay level: Bezahlungsniveau *(n)*; pay loss: Lohnausfall *(m)*; pay office: Lohnbüro *(n)*; pay packet: Lohntüte *(f)*; pay pause: Lohnpause *(f)*; pay per shift: Schichtlohn *(m)*; pay raise ⟨AE⟩: Lohnerhöhung *(f)*; pay rise: Lohnerhöhung *(f)*; pay scale: Lohnskala *(f)*; pay scale/wages regulations *(Pl)*: Tarifforderung *(f)*; pay schedule: Gehaltstabelle *(f)*; pay sheet: Lohn-/Gehaltsliste *(f)*; pay slip: Lohnstreifen *(m)*, Lohnabrechnung *(f)*; pay structure: Lohngefüge *(n)*.

payday — Zahltag *(m)*.

payment — Bezahlung *(f)*, Vergütung *(f)*; payment by results: Ergebnislohn *(m)*,

Leistungsentlohnung *(f)*; payment during leave: Urlaubsentgelt *(n)*; payment in advance: Vorauszahlung *(f)*; payment in part: Teilzahlung *(f)*; payment of damages: Schadenersatzleistung *(f)*; payment on account: (Lohn-)Abschlag *(m)*, Vorschußzahlung *(f)*.

payroll — Lohn-/Gehaltsabrechnung *(f)* ⟨Vorgang⟩; be on the payroll of: beschäftigt sein bei; payroll account: Lohnkonto *(n)*; payroll accounting/bookkeeping: Lohnrechnung *(f)*; payroll department: Lohnbüro *(n)*; payroll tax ⟨AE⟩: Lohnsummensteuer *(f)*; payroll total: Lohnsumme *(f)*.

peak — Gipfel *(m)*, Spitze *(f)*, Höhepunkt *(m)*; peak load: Spitzenbelastung *(f)*; peak performance: Spitzenleistung *(f)*; peak prosperity: Hochkonjunktur *(f)*.

pecuniary aid — finanzieller Zuschuß *(m)*.

pegged wages — Indexlohn *(m)*.

penny fee ⟨BE⟩ — Hungerlohn *(m)*.

pension (off) *(v)* — jmd. pensionieren; pension fund: Pensionsfond *(m)*, Pensionskasse *(f)*; pension liability: Ruhegeldverpflichtung *(f)*; pension plan: Pensionsplan *(m)*; pension reserve: Pensionsrückstellung *(f)*.

pensionable *(adj)* — pensionsfähig, pensionsberechtigt; pensionable age: Pensionsalter *(n)*.

pensionary — Pensionsempfänger(in) *(m ⟨f⟩)*.

pensioner — Pensionär(in) *(m ⟨f⟩)*.

pep ⟨colloq.⟩ — Initiative *(f)*, Elan *(m)*.

per diem allowance — Tagegeld *(n)*, Tagessatz *(m)*.

performance — Leistung *(f)*, Arbeit *(f)*; performance allowance: Leistungszulage *(f)*; performance appraisal: Leistungsbeurteilung *(f)*; performance bond ⟨AE⟩: Leistungsgarantie *(f)*; performance evaluation: Leistungsbewertung *(f)*; performance guarantee: Leistungsgarantie *(f)*; performance level: Leistungsgrad *(m)*; performance principle: Leistungsprinzip *(n)*; performance rating: Leistungsgradschätzung *(f)*; performance report: Arbeitsbericht *(m)*; performance system: Leistungssystem *(n)*.

period — Zeitraum *(m)*, Zeitspanne *(f)*; period of closure: Sperrfrist *(f)*; period of limitation: Verjährungsfrist *(f)*; period of termination: Kündigungsfrist *(f)*; period of vocational adjustment: Einarbeitungszeit *(f)*.

permanent *(adj)* — dauerhaft, andauernd; permanent employment/occupation: Dauerbeschäftigung *(f)*; permanent incapacity: Invalidität *(f)*; permanent position: Dauerstellung *(f)*; permanent post: Dauerstellung *(f)*; permanent staff: Stammpersonal *(n)*.

permit of residence — Zuzugsgenehmigung *(f)*, Aufenthaltsgenehmigung *(f)*.

perquisites *(Pl)* ⟨*BE*⟩ — Nebeneinkünfte *(Pl)*, besondere Bezüge *(Pl)*.

persistent unemployment — Dauerarbeitslosigkeit *(f)*.

person undergoing practical training — Praktikant(in) *(m* ⟨*f*⟩*)*.

personal *(adj)* — persönlich, individuell; personal data *(Pl)*: Personaldaten *(n, Pl)*, Personalangaben *(f, Pl)*; personal earnings *(Pl)*: Arbeitseinkommen *(n)*; personal file: Personalakte *(f)*; personal history: Werdegang *(m)*, Lebenslauf *(m)*; personal protection device: Personensicherungsgerät *(n)*.

personalia *(Pl)* — Personalangaben *(f, Pl)*.

personnel — Personal *(n)*, Belegschaft *(f)*; personnel administration: Personalverwaltung *(f)*; personnel department: Personalabteilung *(f)*; personnel ex-

penditure *(Sg)*: Personalkosten *(Pl)*; personnel expenses *(Pl)*: Personalaufwendungen *(f, Pl)*; personnel index: Personalkartei *(f)*; personnel management: Personalführung *(f)*; personnel manager: Personalleiter *(m)*, Personalchef *(m)*; personnel matter *(Pl)*: Personalangelegenheiten *(f, Pl)*; personnel office: Personalabteilung *(f)*, Personalbüro *(n)*; personnel officer: Personalsachbearbeiter(in) *(m* ⟨*f*⟩*)*; personnel periodical: Betriebszeitung *(f)*, Mitarbeiterzeitschrift *(f)*; personnel policy: Personalpolitik *(f)*; personnel questionnaire: Personalfragebogen *(m)*; personnel record: Personalakte *(f)*; personnel reduction: Personalabbau *(m)*; personnel selection: Personalauswahl *(f)*; personnel strength: Personalstärke *(f)*; personnel-intensive *(adj)*: personalintensiv.

phase of production — Produktionsgang *(m)*.

physical *(adj)* — körperlich.

picket — Streikposten *(m)*; picket line: Streikpostenkette *(f)*.

picketing — Streikpostenstehen *(n)*; secondary picketing: Streikposten vor einem Drittbetrieb stehen/aufstellen, um eigenen Streik zu unterstützen.

piece (rate) worker — Akkordarbeiter *(m)*.

piece rate bonus — Akkordprämie *(f)*.

piece rate formula — Akkordsatz *(m)*.

piece rate pay — Akkordentlohnung *(f)*.

piece wage — Stücklohn *(m)*.

piecework — Akkord *(m)*; piecework bonus: Akkordzuschlag *(m)*; piecework earnings *(Pl)*: Akkordverdienst *(m)*; piecework pay: Akkordbezahlung *(f)*; piecework system: Akkordsystem *(n)*.

pitman — Grubenarbeiter *(m)*, Bergmann *(m)*.

pittancy — Hungerlohn *(m)*.

place *(v)* **a time limiton** — befristen.

place of abode — Wohnsitz *(m)*.

place of work — Arbeitsplatz *(m)*, Arbeitsort.

placement — Arbeitseinsatz *(m)*, Arbeits(platz)zuweisung *(f)*; placement agency: Stellenvermittlung *(f)*.

plant — Fabrik-/Betriebsanlage *(f)*; plant closing: Betriebsstillegung *(f)*; plant health insurance: Betriebskrankenkasse *(f)*; plant management: Betriebsleitung *(f)*; plant manager ⟨AE⟩: Betriebsleiter *(m)*; plant relocation: Betriebsverlegung *(f)*; plant security: Werksicherheit *(f)*, Werkschutz *(m)* ⟨*Sicherung der Anlagen*⟩; plant shutdown: Betriebsruhe *(f)*, Betriebsferien *(Pl)*; plant site: Betriebsgelände *(n)*; plant tour/visit: Betriebsbesichtigung *(f)*, Betriebsrundgang *(m)*.

pleadings *(Pl)* — Prozeßakten *(f, Pl)*, vorbereitende Schriftsätze *(m, Pl)*.

pluck *(v)* ⟨BE⟩ ⟨colloq.⟩ — jmd. bei Prüfung durchfallen lassen; be plucked *(v)* ⟨BE⟩: durchfallen, durchrasseln.

plumber — Klempner *(m)*.

poaching of staff — Abwerbung *(f)* ⟨*Belegschaftsangehörige*⟩.

police report — Vorstrafenregister *(n)*.

population register — Einwohnermeldeamt *(n)*.

porter — Pförtner *(m)*.

portion of wage — Lohnanteil *(m)*.

position — Anstellung *(f)*, Position *(f)*, Posten *(m)*; position analysis: Arbeits-/Stellenanalyse *(f)*; position description: Arbeitsplatzbeschreibung *(f)*; position evaluation: Arbeits(platz)bewertung *(f)*; position of trust: Vertrauensstellung *(f)*; position offered: Stellenangebot *(n)*.

post — Position *(f)*, Posten *(m)*, Stelle *(f)*; post offer: Stellenangebot *(n)*.

postal ballot — Briefwahl *(f)*.

power — Vollmacht *(f)*; power of attorney: Prozeßvollmacht *(f)*; power of procuration: Prokura *(f)*.

practical training (course) — Praktikum *(n)*.

pre-retirement — Vorruhestand *(m)*.

pre-selection — Vorauswahl *(f)*.

precaution(ary) measure — Schutzmaßnahme *(f)*.

predetermined-elemental-time standards — Systeme *(n, Pl)* vorbestimmter Zeiten.

preferential tariff — Sondertarif *(m)*.

pregnancy — Schwangerschaft *(f)*.

premium — Prämie *(f)*, Zuschlag *(m)*, Belohnung *(f)*, Gratifikation *(f)*; premium pay: Prämie *(f)*, Sonderzahlung *(f)*.

prescription — Verjährung *(f)* ⟨*Besitzrecht*⟩.

presentation of an award — Prämiierung *(f)*.

pevarication — Amtspflichtverletzung *(f)*.

previous conviction — Vorstrafe *(f)*.

previously convicted *(adj)* — vorbestraft.

priciple of equity — Billigkeitsgrundsatz *(m)*.

primary education — Grundschul(aus)-bildung *(f)*.

principal *(adj)* — führend, hauptsächlich; principal occupation: Haupttätigkeit *(f)*; principal of equal treatment: Gleichbehandlungsgrundsatz *(m)*; principal shareholder: Großaktionär *(m)*; principal stockholder ⟨AE⟩: Großaktionär *(m)*.

principles for leave arrangements — Urlaubsgrundsätze *(m, Pl)*.

private lessons *(Pl)* — Einzelunterricht *(m)*.

prize — Preis *(m)* ⟨*Auszeichnung*⟩, Prämie *(f)*.

probation (period) — Bewährungszeit *(f)*, Probezeit *(f)*.

probationary employment — Probearbeitsverhältnis *(n)*; probationary period/term: Bewährungszeit *(f)*, Probezeit *(f)*.

procedural law — Prozeßrecht *(n)*.

procedure — Verfahren *(n)*, Verfahrensanweisung *(f)*; code/rules *(Pl)* of procedure: Prozeßordnung *(f)*.

process — Arbeitsgang *(m)*; process of selection: Ausleseverfahren *(n)*.

processing system — Bearbeitungssystem *(n)*.

procuration — Prokura *(f)*, Handlungsvollmacht *(f)*.

procurement of work — Arbeitsvermittlung *(f)*.

produce *(v)* — herstellen, fertigen; producing firm: Produktionsbetrieb *(m)*; producing industry/industries *(Pl)*: produzierendes Gewerbe *(n)*; producing sector: Produktionsbereich *(m)*.

production — Produktion *(f)*, Erzeugung *(f)*, Produktionsmenge *(f)*; production capacity: Produktionskapazität *(f)*; production cost(s): Fertigungskosten *(Pl)*; production cycle: Arbeitstakt *(m)*; production equipment: Fertigungseinrichtungen *(f, Pl)*; production facilities *(Pl)*: Fabrikationseinrichtung *(f)*; production line: Fertigungsstraße *(f)*, Produktionsband *(n)*; production manager: Fertigungsleiter *(m)*, Produktionsleiter *(m)*; production process: Fertigungsverfahren *(n)*; production quota: Produktionssoll *(n)*; production rate: Produktions-

ziffer *(f)*; production target: Produktionsziel *(n)*; production worker: Produktionsarbeiter(in) *(m* ⟨*f*⟩*)*.

productive *(adj)* — leistungsfähig, produktiv; productive equipment: Fabrikationseinrichtung *(f)*; productive wages *(Pl)* — Fertigungslöhne *(m, Pl)*.

productivity — Produktivität *(f)*; produktivity bonus: Produktivitätszulage *(f)*; productivity ceiling/limit: Produktivitätsgrenze *(f)*.

profession — (höherer) Beruf *(m)*.

professional — Fachmann *(m)*.

professional *(adj)* — fachlich, fachmännisch, beruflich; professional association: Berufsverband *(m)*; professional ban: Berufsverbot *(n)*; professional education: Berufsausbildung *(f)*; professional ethics *(Pl)*: Berufsauffassung *(f)*; professional magazine: Fachzeitschrift *(f)*; professional prospects *(Pl)*: Berufsaussichten *(f, Pl)*; professional representation: Berufsvertretung *(f)*; professional school: Fachschule *(f)*; professional training: Fachschulbildung *(f)*.

profit — Gewinn *(m)*; clear profit: Nettogewinn *(m)*; profit sharing: Gewinnbeteiligung *(f)*.

progress sharing — Erfolgsbeteiligung *(f)*.

prohibition of strike(s) — Streikverbot *(n)*.

promote *(v)* **(to the position of)** — befördern zu.

promotion — Förderung *(f)*, Beförderung *(f)* ⟨*eines Arbeitnehmers*⟩; promotional examination: Doktorexamen *(n)*.

prone *(adj)* **to disease** — krankheitsanfällig.

property manager — Immobilienverwalter *(m)*.

prospective managers *(Pl)* — Führungsnachweis *(m)*.

protecting mask — Schutzmaske *(f)*.

protection — Schutz *(m)*, Sicherung *(f)*; Protection Against Dismissal Act: Kündigungsschutzgesetz *(n)*; protection against unlawful dismissal: Kündigungsschutz *(m)*; protection against unwarranted notice: Kündigungsschutz *(m)*; protection fence: Schutzgitter *(n)*; protection of minorities: Minderheitenschutz *(m)*; protection of mothers: Mutterschutz *(m)*.

protective *(adj)* — schützend; protective clause: Schutzklausel *(f)*; protective clothing: Schutz(be)kleidung *(f)*; protective covering: Schutzhülle *(f)*; protective glove: Schutzhandschuh *(m)*; protective grid: Schutzgitter *(n)*; protective hood: Schutzhelm *(m)*, Schutzhaube *(f)*; protective labor legislation *⟨AE⟩*: Arbeitsschutzgesetzgebung *(f)*;

protective sheating: Schutzhülle *(f)*; protective shutter: Schutzgitter *(n)*; protective suit: Schutzanzug *(m)*; protective switch: Schutzschalter *(m)*.

protest strike — Proteststreik *(m)*.

prove o.s. *(v)* — sich bewähren.

provisional order — einstweilige Verfügung *(f)*.

proxy — Prokura *(f)*, Vollmacht *(f)*.

public *(adj)* — öffentlich, staatlich, offenkundig; public assistance *⟨AE⟩*: Sozialhilfe *(f)*; public school: Gymnasium *(n)*; public service *⟨AE⟩*: Staatsdienst *(m)*.

purchasing power — Kaufkraft *(f)* *⟨des Geldes⟩*; purchasing power allowance: Kaufkraftausgleich *(m)*.

put *(v)* **on the sick list** — krankschreiben.

Q

qualification — Eignung *(f)*, Befähigung *(f)*, Anwartschaft *(f)*; qualification test: Eignungsprüfung *(f)*.

qualified *(adj)* — geeignet, qualifiziert; qualified worker: Fachkraft *(f)*.

qualifying examination — Eignungsprüfung *(f)*.

qualifying period — Anwartschaftszeit *(f)*, Karenzzeit *(f)*.

quality — Qualität *(f)*; quality bonus: Qualitätsprämie *(f)*.

quarterly statement of accounts *(Pl)* — Quartalsabrechnung *(f)*.

querulous person — Querulant(in) *(m ⟨f⟩)*.

questionnaire — Fragebogen *(m)*.

quit *(v)* **one's job** — kündigen *⟨vom Arbeitnehmer aus⟩*.

R

raise *⟨AE⟩* — Lohnzulage *(f)*.

range of validity — Gültigkeitsbereich *(m)*.

range of wage(s) — Lohnspanne *(f)*.

rank — Rang *(m)*, Grad *(m)*, Stufe *(f)*; rank order: Rangordnung *(f)*.

rank-and-file — Arbeiterschaft *(f)*, „die breite Masse" *⟨Ausdr.⟩*, Mannschaft *(f)*.

ranking — Rangfolge *(f)*, Rangordnung *(f)*.

rate *(v)* — bewerten, beurteilen.

rate of advance — Steigerungsbetrag *(m)*.

rate setting — Vorgabezeitermittlung *(f)*, Lohnfestsetzung *(f)*.

rating — Bewertung *(f)*, Beurteilung *(f)*.

rationalization — Rationalisierung *(f)*.

re-classification — Lohn-/Gehaltsgruppenumstufung *(f)*.

re-education — Umschulung *(f)*.

re-employment — Wiederbeschäftigung *(f)*, Wiedereinstellung *(f)*.

re-instatement — Wiedereinstellung *(f)*.

ready money — Bargeld *(n)*.

reappointment — Wiedereinstellung *(f)*.

rebate — Rabatt *(m)*.

receipt in full discharge — Ausgleichsquittung *(f)*.

receive *(v)* **one's notice** — gekündigt werden.

recess ⟨*AE*⟩ — Arbeitspause *(f)*.

recession — Konjunkturabschwächung *(f)*.

reciprocal *(adj)* — gegenseitig.

reclamation — Beschwerde *(f)*.

reconciliation — Schlichtung *(f)*; reconciliation of interests: Interessenausgleich *(m)*.

record — Leumund *(m)*, Bericht *(m)*, Protokoll *(n)*, Urkunde *(f)*.

recourse — Regreß *(m)*.

recovery — Erholung *(f)*, Wiedereingewöhnung *(f)*.

recreation — Erholung *(f)*, Arbeitsruhe *(f)*; recreation facility: Freizeiteinrichtung *(f)*; recreation room: Ruheraum *(m)*, Gemeinschaftsraum *(m)*; recreation service: Freizeitgestaltungsprogramm *(n)*; recreation time: Erhol(ungs)zeit *(f)*; recreational program(me): Erholungsprogramm *(n)*.

recruit *(v)* ⟨*AE*⟩ — Personal beschaffen/einstellen.

recruitment ⟨*AE*⟩ — Personalbeschaffung *(f)*, Personaleinstellung *(f)*.

redemption money — Abgeltungsbetrag *(m)*.

redirect *(v)* — umbestellen.

reduced output — Minderleistung *(f)*.

reduction — Verminderung *(f)*, Abbau *(m)*, Rabatt *(m)*; reduction of wages/pay: Lohnabbau *(m)*; reduction of working hours: Arbeitszeitverkürzung *(f)*.

redundancy — Personalüberschuß *(m)*; redundancy payment: Abfindung *(f)* ⟨*für Verlust des Arbeitsplatzes*⟩; redundancy scheme: Abfindungsplan *(m)*.

redundant labo(u)r — Arbeitskräfteüberschuß *(m)*.

refinement — Kultiviertheit *(f)*, feine Bildung *(f)*.

refresher course — Fortbildungslehrgang *(m)*.

refund(ment) — Rückerstattung *(f)*.

refusal to work — Arbeitsverweigerung *(f)*.

register of employe(e)s — Personalverzeichnis *(n)*, Personalkartei *(f)*.

registrar — Registrator(in) *(m* ⟨*f*⟩*)*.

registration certificate — Aufenthaltserlaubnis *(f)* ⟨*Ausländer*⟩.

registration office — Einwohnermeldeamt *(n)*.

regrading — Umgruppierung *(f)*.

regress — Regreß *(m)*.

regular pay/wage — Normallohn *(m)*.

rehiring — Wiedereinstellung *(f)*.

reimbursement — Rückerstattung *(f)*.

relaxation — Entspannung *(f)*, Erholung *(f)*.

release — Entlastung *(f)*, Befreiung *(f)*, Freistellung *(f)*, Entlassung *(f)*; release *(v)* from work: jmd. von der Arbeit freistellen; release from work(ing): Arbeitsfreistellung *(f)*, Arbeitsbefreiung.

relief — Unterstützung *(f)*, Entlastung *(f)*, Fürsorge *(f)*; relief man: Springer *(m)*; relief program(me): Arbeitsbeschaffungsprogramm *(n)*; relief time: (persönliche) Verteilzeit *(f)*.

relocate *(v)* — verlegen ⟨örtlich⟩, verlagern.

relocation — Verlegung *(f)*, Verlagerung *(f)*, Umzug *(m)*.

remainder — Restbetrag *(m)*, Anwartschaft *(f)*.

remedial instruction — Förder(ungs)unterricht *(m)*.

removal — Umzug *(m)*, Verlegung *(f)*, Amtsenthebung *(f)*; removal allowance ⟨BE⟩: Umzugskostenhilfe *(f)*; removal expenses *(Pl)*: Umzugskosten *(Pl)*.

remove *(v)* — umziehen.

remuneration — Vergütung *(f)*, Entlohnung *(f)*, Bezahlung *(f)*; remuneration for employe(e) inventions: Erfindervergütung *(f)*; remuneration principle: Entlohnungsgrundsatz *(m)*.

rent allowance — Mietzuschuß *(m)*.

repairman — Mechaniker *(m)* ⟨Auto, Flugzeug⟩.

repayment — Rückerstattung *(f)*.

replacement — Ersatzbeschaffung *(f)*, Ersatzeinstellung *(f)*; replacement needs *(Pl)*: Ersatzbedarf *(m)*.

report — Bericht *(m)*, Beurteilung *(f)*, Gutachten *(n)*.

reportable *(adj)* — anzeigepflichtig; reportable accident: meldepflichtiger Unfall *(m)*.

representation of juvenile employees — Jugendvertretung *(f)*.

representation of the personnel/staff — Personalvertretung *(f)*.

reprimand — Verwarnung *(f)*, Verweis *(m)*, Maßregelung *(f)*.

reproof — Verweis *(m)*.

repudiation — Leistungsverweigerung *(f)*.

reputation — Leumund *(m)*.

request — Forderung *(f)*.

reserve officer — Reserveoffizier *(m)*.

resettlement — ⟨soziale⟩ Wiedereingliederung *(f)*.

residence — Wohnsitz *(m)*; residence permit: Aufenthaltserlaubnis *(f)*.

residential allowance — Ortszuschlag *(m)*.

respond *(v)* ⟨AE⟩ — haften.

responsibility — Verantwortung *(f)*, Pflicht *(f)*, Aufgabe *(f)*, Haftung *(f)*.

responsible *(adj)* — verantwortlich.

rest — Ruhepause *(f)*, Pause *(f)*; rest cure: Erholungskur *(f)*; rest period: Erholungspause *(f)*; rest period requirement: Erholungsbedarf *(m)*; rest time: Erholzeit *(f)*.

restraint clause — Konkurrenzklausel *(f)*, Wettbewerbsklausel *(f)*.

restraint of trade — Wettbewerbsverbot *(n)*.

restriction — Einschränkung *(f)*, Begrenzung *(f)*.

result wage — Erfolgslohn *(m)*.

resume — Werdegang *(m)*, Lebenslauf *(m)*.

resume *(v)* **work** — Arbeit wiederaufnehmen.

retainer — Prozeßvollmacht *(f)*.

retention — Einbehaltung *(f)*; right of retention: Zurückbehaltungsrecht.

retire *(v)* — jmd. in den Ruhestand versetzen, pensionieren, zurücktreten, in den Ruhestand treten.

retired pay — Ruhegehalt *(n)*, Pension *(f)*, Altersrente *(f)*.

retirement — Ruhestand *(m)*, Pensionierung *(f)*; retirement age: Pensionsalter *(n)*; retirement fund: Pensionskasse *(f)*; retirement pension: Ruhegehalt *(n)*, Altersrente *(f)*; retirement provisions: Altersfürsorge *(f)*.

retraining — Umschulung *(f)*.

retroactive payment of wages — Lohnnachzahlung *(f)*.

reversionary *(adj)* — anwartschaftlich.

reward — Belohnung *(f)*, Honorar *(n)*.

right — Anrecht *(n)*, Anspruch *(m)*; customary right: Gewohnheitsrecht *(n)*; right of co-determination: Mitbestimmungsrecht *(n)*; right of retention: Zurückbehaltungsrecht *(n)*; right to a pension: Pensionsanspruch *(m)*; right to be heard: Anhörungsrecht *(n)* ⟨*des Betriebsrats*⟩; right to conclude collective agreements: Tarifhoheit *(f)*; right to form unions and associations/coalitions: Koalitionsfreiheit *(f)*; right to give notice: Kündigungsrecht *(n)*; right to information/be notified: Informationsrecht *(n)*; right to refuse to give evidence: Zeugnisverweigerungsrecht *(n)*; right to strike: Streikrecht *(n)*.

ringleader — Rädelsführer *(m)*.

rise in pay/salary ⟨*colloq.*⟩ — Gehaltserhöhung *(f)*.

rise in wages — Lohnanstieg *(m)*.

rival — Mitbewerber *(m)*.

rough *(adj)* — grob ⟨*Arbeit*⟩.

round of wage negotiations — Lohnrunde *(f)*.

routing slip — Laufzettel *(m)*.

rule — Grundsatz *(m)*, Regel *(f)*; rules *(Pl)* of procedure: Prozeßordnung *(f)*.

run *(v)* **an operation** — einen Betrieb leiten.

running period — Laufzeit *(f)*, Gültigkeitsdauer *(f)*.

S

sack *(v)* ⟨*colloq.*⟩ — jmd. entlassen.

safety — Sicherheit *(f)*, Schutz *(m)*; safety facility: Sicherheitseinrichtung *(f)*; safety goggles *(Pl)*: Schutzbrille *(f)*; safety guard: Schutzgitter *(n)*; safety helmet: Schutzhelm *(m)*; safety regulations: Unfallverhütungsvorschriften *(f, Pl)*, Sicherheitsbestimmungen *(f, Pl)*.

salaried employe(e) — Gehaltsempfänger(in) *(m* ⟨*f*⟩*)*, Angestellte(r) *(f* ⟨*m*⟩*)*; salaried employe(e) representation: Angestelltenvertretung *(f)*.

salaried employment (status) — Angestelltenverhältnis *(n)*.

salary *(v)* — besolden.

salary — Besoldung *(f)*, Gehalt *(n)*; initial salary: Anfangsgehalt *(n)*; salary account: Gehaltskonto *(n)*; salary adjustment: Gehaltsanpassung *(f)*; salary administration: Gehaltsverwaltung *(f)*; salary advance: Gehaltsvorschuß *(m)*; salary bonus: Gehaltszulage *(f)*; salary grade: Gehaltsgruppe *(f)*; salary increase: Gehaltserhöhung *(f)*; salary role: Gehaltsliste *(f)*; salary scale: Gehaltstabelle *(f)*; salary slip: Gehaltsabrechnung *(f)*, Gehaltsstreifen *(m)*; salary structure agreement: Gehaltsrahmentarifvertrag *(m)*.

sales agent — Handelsvertreter *(m)*.

sanitation — Heilfürsorge *(f)*.

satisfy *(v)* — entschädigen, abfinden.

saving — Einsparung *(f)*; savings premium: Sparprämie *(f)*.

scab *⟨colloq.⟩* — Streikbrecher *(m)*.

scabwork — Schwarzarbeit *(f)*.

scale of wages/salaries — Tarif *(m)*, Lohn-/Gehaltsstaffel *(f)*.

scale-wage employe(e) — Tarifangestellte(r) *(f ⟨m⟩)*.

scarce job — Mangelberuf *(m)*.

scarcity — Mangel *(m)*, Knappheit *(f)*.

scholarship — Stipendium *(n)*.

school-leaving — Schulabgang *(m)*.

scope — Gültigkeitsbereich *(m)* *⟨eines Gesetzes⟩*; scope of activities *(Pl)*: Wirkungsbereich *(m)*.

screening system — Ausleseverfahren *(n)*.

seasonal worker — Saisonarbeiter *(m)*.

secondary agreement — Nebenabrede *(f)*.

secrecy — Verschwiegenheit *(f)*.

secretary (to s.o.) — Sekretär(in) *(m ⟨f⟩)* (von jmd.).

section — Abteilung *(f)* *⟨einer Verwaltung⟩*; section chief: Abteilungsleiter(in) *(m ⟨f⟩)*.

sectional meeting — Teilversammlung *(f)*.

security control — Sicherheits(über)-prüfung *(f)*, Torkontrolle *(f)*.

select *(v)* — auswählen.

selection — Auswahl *(f)*; selection guideline: Auswahlrichtlinie *(f)*; selection test: Auswahltest *(m)*.

selective employment tax *⟨BE⟩* — Lohnsummensteuer *(f)*.

selective strike — Schwerpunktstreik *(m)*.

self-appraisal — Selbsteinschätzung *(f)*.

self-rating — Selbstbeurteilung *(f)*.

semi-skilled *(adj)* — angelernt; semi-skilled occupation: Anlernberuf *(m)*.

senior clerk — Bürovorsteher(in) *(m ⟨f⟩)*.

senior staff — Betriebsleitung *(f)*.

seniority *⟨AE⟩* — Dienstalter *(n)*; seniority system: Dienstaltersprinzip *(n)*.

separation allowance — Trennungszulage *(f)*.

separation payment — Abfindung *(f)* *⟨für Verlust des Arbeitsplatzes⟩*.

seperate department — Betriebsteil *(m)*.

sequence of operations — (techn.) Arbeitsablauf *(m)*.

series of strikes *(Pl)* — Streikwelle *(f)*.

seriously disabled person — Schwerbehinderte(r) *(f ⟨m⟩)*.

serve *(v)* — dienen, arbeiten; serve one's apprenticeship: im Lehrverhältnis *(n)* stehen, lernen.

service — Dienst *(m)*.

session — Unterrichtsstunde *(f)*, Kursus *(m)*.

settle *(v)* — vereinbaren, sich einigen, aushandeln, erledigen.

settlement — Vereinbarung *(f)*, Abschluß *(m)*, Vergleich *(m)*; settlement of hardship cases: Härteregelung *(f)*.

severance pay — Entlassungsabfindung *(f)*.

severity allowance — Erschwerniszulage *(f)*.

share — Anteil *(m)*; give *(v)* s.o. a share: jmd. mitbeteiligen; share in profits *(Pl)*: Gewinnbeteiligung *(f)*; share in wages: Lohnanteil *(m)*; share savings scheme: Wertpapierersparnis *(m)*.

shareholder ⟨BE⟩ — Anteilseigner *(m)*, Aktionär *(m)*; shareholder representative: Aktionärsvertreter *(m)* ⟨im Aufsichtsrat⟩.

shelter — Notunterkunft *(f)*.

shift — Arbeitsschicht *(f)*; shift changeover/rotation: planmäßiger Schichtwechsel *(m)*; shift in the staff/personnel: Personalwechsel *(m)*; shift pay: Schichtlohn *(m)*; shift premium/allowance: Schichtzulage *(f)*; shift schedule: Schichtplan *(m)*; shift work: Schichtarbeit *(f)*; shift worker: Schichtarbeiter(in) *(m ⟨f⟩)*.

shift(ing) — Umbesetzung *(f)*.

ship's committee — Bordvertretung *(f)*.

shop regulations *(Pl)* — Arbeitsordnung *(f)*.

shop steward — Vertrauensmann *(m)* im Betrieb, Gewerkschaftsbeauftragter *(m)*.

shopworker ⟨AE⟩ — Maschinenarbeiter(in) *(m ⟨f⟩)*.

short leave — Kurzurlaub *(m)*.

short-time work(ing) — Kurzarbeit *(f)*, Betriebseinschränkung *(f)*; short-time worker: Kurzarbeiter(in) *(m ⟨f⟩)*.

short-timer — Kurzarbeiter(in) *(m ⟨f⟩)*.

shortage — Mangel *(m)*, Knappheit *(f)*; shortage of personnel: Personalmangel *(m)*.

shortened work-week allowance — Kurzarbeiterunterstützung *(f)*.

shorthand (writing) — Kurzschrift *(f)*; shorthand clerk: Stenokontorist(in)

(m ⟨f⟩); shorthand note: Stenogramm *(n)*.

shuggard — Faulenzer *(m)*.

shutdown — Betriebsferien *(Pl)*, Betriebsruhe *(f)*.

shuttle bus — Pendlerbus *(m)*.

sick *(adj)* — krank, unwohl; sick fund: Krankenkasse *(f)*; sick leave: Krankheitsurlaub *(m)*, Erholungsurlaub *(m)*; sick list: Krankenliste *(f)*; be *(v)* on the sick list: krankgeschrieben sein; put *(v)* on the sick list: krankschreiben; sick nurse: Krankenschwester *(f)*.

sickness — Krankheit *(f)*, Übelkeit *(f)*; sickness allowance: Krankenbeihilfe *(f)*; sickness benefit ⟨BE⟩: Krankengeld *(n)*; sickness insuranc fund/plan ⟨AE⟩: Krankenkasse *(f)*.

sickpay — Krankengeld *(n)*.

sideline employment — Nebenberuf *(m)*.

sign off *(v)* — kündigen ⟨arbeitnehmerseitig⟩.

sign-in — Unterschriftensammlung *(f)*.

signing clerk — Prokurist *(m)*.

signing power — Unterschriftsvollmacht *(f)*.

silent *(adj)* — stillschweigend.

single *(adj)* — ledig, allein(stehend); single procuration: Einzelprokura *(f)*; single shift operation: Einschichtbetrieb *(m)*.

skeleton — Rahmen *(m)*, Gerippe *(n)*, Gerüst *(n)*; skeleton agreement: Rahmenabkommen *(n)*; skeleton contract: Rahmenvertrag *(m)*; skeleton law: Rahmengesetz *(n)*.

skill — (Fach-)Können *(n)*; skilled operative/worker: ausgebildete(r) Arbeiter(in) *(m ⟨f⟩)*, Facharbeiter(in) *(m ⟨f⟩)*; skilled staff/personnel: Fachpersonal *(n)*.

slack *(v)* **at one's work** — bei der Arbeit bummeln.

get *(v)* **slacked** — gekündigt werden.

slacker — Drückeberger *(m)*.

slow down — Arbeitsverzögerung *(f)*, Bummelstreik *(m)*, bewußtes Langsamarbeiten *(n)*.

sociable *(adj)* — kontaktfähig.

social *(adj)* — sozial, gesellschaftlich; social (compensation) plan: Sozialplan *(m)*; social economic balance sheet: Sozialbilanz *(f)*; social expenditure: Sozialaufwand *(m)*, Sozialleistungen *(f, Pl)*; social insurance: Sozialversicherung *(f)*; social insurance contribution: Sozialversicherungsbeitrag *(m)*; social security ⟨AE⟩: Sozialversicherung *(f)*; social security contibution ⟨AE⟩: Sozialversicherungsbeitrag *(m)*, Sozialabgaben *(f, Pl)*; social service: Fürsorge *(f)*; social services *(Pl)*: Sozialeinrichtung *(f)*; social welfare: Sozialhilfe *(f)*.

sociology — Soziologie *(f)*.

sole *(adj)* — alleinstehend; sole procuration: Einzelprokura *(f)*.

solvency — Zahlungsfähigkeit *(f)*, finanzielle Leistungsfähigkeit *(f)*.

solvent *(adj)* — zahlungsfähig.

sparetime — Freizeit *(f)*.

special *(adj)* — besonders, ausdrücklich, außergewöhnlich; special agreement: Sondervereinbarung *(f)*; special allowance: Funktionszulage *(f)*; special bonus: Sondervergütung *(f)*, Sonderzulage *(f)*; special knowlege: Fachkenntnisse *(f, Pl)*; special leave: Sonderurlaub *(m)*; special licence/license ⟨AE⟩/permit: Sondergenehmigung *(f)*; special meeting: Sondersitzung *(f)*; special provision/stipulation: Sonderbestimmung *(f)*; special school for educationally subnormal children: Sonderschule *(f)*, Hilfsschule *(f)*; special services *(Pl)*: Sonderleistungen *(f, Pl)*; special session: Sondersitzung *(f)*; special subject: Hauptfach *(n)* ⟨in der Schule⟩; special training: Fachausbildung *(f)*.

specialist — Fachmann *(m)*.

speciality — Hauptfach *(n)*.

specialized *(adj)* — fachmännisch.

specification — Einzelnachweis *(m)*.

specimen of one's handwriting — Handschriftenprobe *(f)*.

spending power — Kaufkraft *(f)* ⟨der Konsumenten⟩.

sphere of action — Aufgabenbereich *(m)*.

sphere of business — Geschäftsbereich *(m)*, Aufgabenbereich *(m)*.

splitting up — Aufsplitterung *(f)*.

spotless *(adj)* — unbescholten.

spouse — Ehefrau *(f)*.

staff ⟨BE⟩ — Belegschaft *(f)*, Personal *(n)*; clerical staff: Büropersonal *(n)*; staff department: Betriebsabteilung *(f)*; staff member: Betriebsangehörige(r) *(m* ⟨f⟩*)*, Mitarbeiter(in) *(m* ⟨f⟩*)*; staff outing: Betriebsausflug *(m)*; staff planning/appointment scheme: Stellenplan *(m)*; staff reduction: Personalabbau *(m)*.

stagger *(v)* — staffeln ⟨Arbeitszeit⟩.

stand *(v)* — sich bewerben.

stand-by time — Arbeitsbereitschaft *(f)*.

standard — Normalmaß *(n)*, Maßtab *(m)*; standard (performance): Vorgabeleistung *(f)*; standard elemental times *(Pl)*: Elementarzeiten *(f, Pl)*; standard of performance: Leistungsnorm *(f)*; standard output: Normalleistung *(f)*; standard wage: Tariflohn *(m)*; standard working day: Normalarbeitstag *(m)*; standard working time: Normalarbeitszeit *(f)*.

standstill of production — Produktionseinstellung *(f)*.

starting *(adj)* — Ausgangs-, Anfangs-; starting date: Einstellungstermin *(m)*; starting of work: Dienstantritt *(m)*; starting rate: Anfangslohn *(m)*, Anfangsgehalt *(n)*; starting salary: Anfangsgehalt *(n)*; starting time: Arbeitsbeginn *(m)*.

starvation wages *(Pl)*: Hungerlohn *(m)*.

state of exhaustion — Erschöpfungszustand *(m)*.

state of the economy — Konjunktur *(f)*, wirtschaftliche Lage *(f)*.

statement of functions — Funktionsbeschreibung *(f)*.

statute of limitation(s) — Verjährung *(f)*; come *(v)* under the statute of limitations: verjähren.

statutory *(adj)* — gesetzlich vorgeschrieben.

stay abroad — Auslandsaufenthalt *(m)*.

stenography — Kurzschrift *(f)*.

stipulate *(v)* — vereinbaren.

stipulation — Vereinbarung *(f)*; stipulation in restraint of trade: Konkurrenzklausel *(f)*.

stockholder ⟨*AE*⟩ — Anteilseigner *(m)*, Aktionär *(m)*.

stopgap — Aushilfskraft *(f)*; stopgap aid: Überbrückungsbeihilfe *(f)*.

stoppage — Betriebsausfall *(m)*, Betriebsstillstand *(m)*; stoppage of production: Produktionseinstellung *(f)*.

store-room clerk — Lagerverwalter(in) *(m ⟨f⟩)*.

storeman — Lagerarbeiter *(m)*.

strength of character — Charakterfestigkeit *(f)*.

strict liability — Gefährdungshaftung *(f)*.

strike *(v)* — streiken.

strike — Streik *(m)*; be *(v)* on strike: streiken; come out *(v)* on strike: streiken; strike ballot: Urabstimmung *(f)*; strike benefit: Streikgeld *(n)*, Streikunterstützung *(f)*; strike call: Streikaufruf *(m)*; strike commitee: Streikleitung *(f)*; strike front: Streikfront *(f)*; strike fund: Streikkasse *(f)*, Streikfond *(m)*; strike leader: Streikführer *(m)*; strike movement: Streikbewegung *(f)*; strike order: Streikbefehl *(m)*; strike pay: Streikgeld *(n)*; strike slogan: Streikparole *(f)*; strike threat: Streikdrohung *(f)*; strike vote: Streikabstimmung *(f)*, Urabstimmung *(f)*; strike-prone *(adj)*: streikanfällig.

strikebreaker — Streikbrecher *(m)*; strikebreaker's work: Streikarbeit *(f)*.

striker — Streikender *(m)*.

student aid — Studienbeihilfe *(f)*.

study *(v)* — studieren, lernen.

study — Studium *(n)*.

study leave — Bildungsurlaub *(m)*; study side: Studienrichtung *(f)*.

subordinate — Untergebene(r) *(f ⟨m⟩)*.

subordinate *(adj)* — untergeben, untergeordnet, unterstellt.

subsequent payment — Nachzahlung *(f)*.

subsidiary activity — Nebentätigkeit *(f)*.

subsidy — ⟨*staatlicher*⟩ Zuschuß *(m)*, Unterstützungsleistung *(f)*.

substantiation — Glaubhaftmachung *(f)*.

substitute — Ersatzmitglied *(n)*, Vertreter *(m)*.

substitution — Vertretung *(f)* im Amt.

suggestion — (Verbesserungs-)Vorschlag *(m)*.

suggestion scheme — Vorschlagswesen *(n)*.

suit — Klage *(f)*.

suitability — Eignung *(f)*.

Sunday work(ing) — Sonntagsarbeit *(f)*.

superannuate *(v)* — pensionieren ⟨*aus Altersgründen*⟩.

superannuation — Pension *(f)*; superannuation fund: Pensionskasse *(f)*.

superintendence — Aufsicht *(f)*.

superintendend *(v)* — beaufsichtigen, leiten.

superior — Vorgesetzte(r) *(m* ⟨*f*⟩*)*.

supervision — ⟨*Dienst-*⟩Aufsicht *(f)*.

supervisor — Aufsichtsperson *(f)*; supervisory authority: Aufsichtsbehör-de *(f)*; supervisory board ⟨*of a German-type public limited company*⟩: Aufsichtsrat *(m)*; supervisory employe(e): Vorgesetzte(r) *(f* ⟨*m*⟩*)*.

supplementary *(adj)* — ergänzend; supplementary insurance: Zusatzversicherung *(f)*; supplementary training: Fortbildung *(f)*.

support — Unterhalt *(m)*.

surtax — Ergänzungsabgabe *(f)*.

surveillance — Polizeiaufsicht *(f)*.

sweated money — Hungerlohn *(m)*.

T

tacit *(adj)* — stillschweigend.

take *(v)* one's (doctor's) degree — promovieren.

take-home pay — Nettoverdienst *(m)*.

take-net pay — Nettoverdienst *(m)*.

taker-in — Heimarbeiter(in) *(m* ⟨*f*⟩*)*.

talent — Begabung *(f)*.

talented *(adj)* — begabt.

tariff *(v)* — tariflich.

tariff — Tariftabelle *(f)*; according to/as per tariff: tariflich; tariff agreement: Tarifvertrag *(m)*; tariff area/region: Tarifgebiet *(n)*; tariff claim: Tarifforderung *(f)*; tariff class: Tarifklasse *(f)*; tariff commission: Tarifkommission *(f)*; tariff committee: Tarifausschuß *(m)*; tariff negotiations *(Pl)*: Tarifverhandlungen *(f, Pl)*; tariff policy: Tarifpolitik *(f)*; tariff settlement: Tarifabschluß *(m)*; tariff structure: Tarifstruktur *(f)*; tariff wage group: Tariflohngruppe *(f)*; tariff(ing) system: Tarifsystem *(n)*.

tariff-wise *(adj)* — tariflich.

task — Aufgabe *(f)*, Arbeit *(f)*; task wages *(Pl)*: Stücklohn *(m)*; task worker: Akkordarbeiter *(m)*.

teach *(v)* — lehren, unterrichten.

teaching job/profession — Lehrberuf *(m)*.

team — (Arbeits-)Gruppe *(f)*, Mannschaft *(f)*.

teamwork — Gemeinschaftsarbeit *(f)*.

technique — Verfahren *(n)*.

telltale — Kontrolluhr *(f)*.

temporary *(adj)* — zeitweise, einstweilig; temporary employment on loan basis: Leiharbeitsverhältnis *(n)*; temporay help: Aushilfskraft *(f)*; temporary help/assistance: Aushilfe *(f)*; temporary worker: Zeitarbeiter(in) *(m* ⟨*f*⟩*)*.

term — Frist *(f)*, bestimmte Zeitdauer *(f)*, Ziel *(n)*; come *(v)* to terms on: (endgültig) aushandeln.

term of limitation — Verjährungsfrist *(f)*.

term of termination — Kündigungsfrist *(f)*.

terminable *(adj)* — kündbar ⟨*Vertrag*⟩.

terminableness — Kündbarkeit *(f)*.

terminate *(v)* **one's employment** — kündigen ⟨arbeitgeberseitig⟩.

termination (of employment) — Kündigung *(f)*, Beendigung *(f)* des Arbeitsverhältnisses.

termination pay — Kündigungsabfindung *(f)*.

test — Erprobung *(f)*, Prüfung *(f)*.

testimonial — Dienstzeugnis *(n)*, Führungszeugnis *(n)* für Angestellte.

thesis — Doktorarbeit *(f)*, Diplomarbeit *(f)*.

third-party insurance — Haftpflichtversicherung *(f)*.

time — Zeit *(f)*; time clock: Stempeluhr *(f)*, Stechuhr *(f)*; time limit: Befristung *(f)*; time of apprenticeship: Lehrzeit *(f)*; time of probation: Probezeit*(f)*; time off: Arbeitsbefreiung *(f)*, Arbeitfreistellung *(f)*; give *(v)* s. o. time off: jmd. beurlauben/freistellen; time standard: Vorgabezeit *(f)*; time study: Zeitstudie *(f)*; time study engineer: Zeitstudieningenieur(in) *(m ⟨f⟩)*; time study sheet: Zeitaufnahmebogen *(m)*.

timekeeping — Zeitkontrolle *(f)*.

toolmaker — Werkzeugmacher(in) *(m ⟨f⟩)*.

tools *(Pl)* — Arbeitsmittel *(n, Pl)*.

top — Spitze *(f)*, Gipfel *(m)*; top earner: Spitzenverdiener *(m)*; top efficiency: Spitzenleistung *(f)*, Höchstleistung *(f)*; top management: Führungsspitze *(f)*; top spot/position: Spitzenposition *(f)*.

total *(adj)* — ganz, gesamt; total earnings *(Pl)*: Gesamtverdienst *(m)*; total income: Gesamteinkommen *(n)*; total wages and salaries: Lohn- und Gehaltssumme *(f)*; total output: Gesamtleistung *(f)*; total wages *(Pl)*: Lohnsumme *(f)*; total workforce: Gesamtbelegschaft *(f)*.

trade — Gewerbe *(n)*, Beruf *(m)*, Handel *(m)*, Gewerbetätigkeit *(f)*; Trade Act: Gewerbeordnung *(f)*; trade association: Wirtschaftsvereinigung *(f)*; trade control office: Gewerbeaufsichtsamt *(n)*, Gewerbeaufsichtsbehörde *(f)*; trade cycle: Konjunkturkreislauf *(m)*; trade register: Handelsregister *(n)*; trade regulations *(Pl)*: Gewerberecht *(n)*; trade school: Berufsschule *(f)*; trade secret: Betriebsgeheimnis *(n)*, Geschäftsgeheimnis *(n)*; trade union: Gewerkschaft *(f)*; Trade Union Congress *(TUC)*: Britischer Gewerkschaftsbund; trade unionist: Gewerkschaft(l)er(in) *(m ⟨f⟩)*.

trademaster — Handwerksmeister *(m)*.

train *(v)* **s. o. for** — lehren, unterrichten, jmd. einarbeiten; trained staff: Fachpersonal *(n)*.

trainee — Anlernling *(m)*, Lehrling *(m)*.

training — Ausbildung *(f)*, Lehre *(f)*, Unterweisung *(f)*, Schulung *(f)*; training course: Schulungskurs *(m)*; training grant/subsidy: Ausbildungsbeihilfe *(f)*; training of apprentices: Lehrlingsausbildung *(f)*; training session: Schulungskurs *(m)*; training supervisor: Lehrgangsleiter *(m)*.

transfer *(v)* — (Personal) umsetzen/versetzen; transfer allowance ⟨AE⟩: Umzugskostenbeihilfe *(f)*.

transfer — Versetzung *(f)*, Arbeitsplatzwechsel *(m)* ⟨im Betrieb⟩.

transmission of money — Geldüberweisung *(f)*.

transportation — Beförderung *(f)*, Versendung *(f)*; transportation allowance: Fahrtkostenzuschuß *(m)*; transportation cost refund: Fahrtkostenerstattung *(f)*; transportation pool: Fahrgemeinschaft *(f)*.

travel — Reise *(f)*; travel advance: Reisekostenvorschuß *(m)*; travel expenses *(Pl)*: Reisekosten *(Pl)*; travel on official business: Dienstreise *(f)*; travel time: Reisezeit *(f)*; travel(ing) expenses/charges *(Pl)*: Reisekosten *(Pl)*, Reisespesen *(Pl)*.

treated as equal *(adj)* — gleichgestellt.

trial — Prüfung *(f)*, ⟨Straf-⟩Prozeß *(m)*; trial period: Probezeit *(f)*.

trouble — Mühe *(f)*, Ärger *(m)*; trouble-

shooter: Problemlöser *(m)*, Vermittler *(m)*, Schlichter *(m)*.

true rent — Grundrente *(f)*.

turnover — Wechsel *(m)* zu einem anderen Betrieb, Fluktuation *(f)*; turnover in the personnel/staff: Personalwechsel *(m)*, Fluktuation *(f)*.

tut ⟨BE⟩ — Akkord *(m)*

U

unable *(adj)* to work — arbeitsunfähig.

unemployable *(adj)* — nicht einsetzbar, verwendungsunfähig.

unemployed *(adj)* — arbeitslos, beschäftigungslos; unemployed person: Arbeitslose(r) *(f* ⟨m⟩*)*.

unemployment — Arbeitslosigkeit *(f)*; chronic/persistent unemployment: Dauerarbeitslosigkeit *(f)*; unemployment benefit/pay/compensation: Arbeitslosengeld *(n)*, Arbeitslosenunterstützung *(f)*; unemployment rate: Arbeitslosenquote *(f)*; unemployment relief: Arbeitslosenhilfe *(f)*, Arbeitslosenfürsorge *(f)*; Unemployment-Compensation-Law ⟨AE⟩: Arbeitslosenunterstützungsgesetz; Unemployment-Workman-Act ⟨BE⟩: Arbeitslosenunterstützungsgesetz.

unfilled job offering — Stellenangebot *(n)*.

unfit *(adj)* — unfähig; unfit to work: arbeitsunfähig, berufsunfähig.

unfitness for work — Arbeitsunfähigkeit *(f)*.

ungifted *(adj)* — unbegabt.

unhealthy *(adj)* — gesundheitsschädlich, gesundheitschädigend, ungesund.

union due — Gewerkschaftsbeitrag *(m)*

union official/officer — Gewerkschaftsfunktionär(in) *(m* ⟨f⟩*)*.

union rate — Tariflohn *(m)*.

unionized *(adj)* — gewerkschaftlich organisiert.

unit cost — Stückkosten *(Pl)*.

university — Universität *(f)*, Hochschule *(f)*; university education: Hochschulbildung *(f)*; university graduate: Hochschulabsolvent(in) *(m* ⟨f⟩*)*; university man: Akademiker *(m)*.

unlawful *(adj)* — gesetzwidrig, ungesetzlich.

unmarried *(adj)* — unverheiratet, ledig.

unoccupied *(adj)* — erwerbslos.

unrefinement — Bildungsmangel *(m)*.

unrelated *(adj)* to one's vocation/profession — berufsfremd.

unreliable *(adj)* — unzuverlässig.

unskilled *(adj)* — ungelernt; unskilled worker: ungelernte(r) Arbeiter(in) *(m* ⟨f⟩*)*, Hilfsarbeiter(in) *(m* ⟨f⟩*)*.

untalented *(adj)* — unbegabt.

untrained *(adj)* — ungelernt, unausgebildet.

upward tendency of wages — Lohnauftrieb *(m)*.

V

vacancy — offene Stelle *(f)*.

vacant post — unbesetzte Stelle *(f)*.

vacation ⟨*AE*⟩ — (Erholungs-) Urlaub *(m)*, Ferien *(Pl)*; on vacation: beurlaubt, in Ferien *(Pl)*; vacation benefit/bonus: Urlaubsgeld *(n)*; vacation compensation (pay) ⟨*AE*⟩: Urlaubsentgelt *(n)*; vacation entitlement: Urlaubsanspruch *(m)*; vacation payment: Urlaubsentgelt *(n)*; vacation period: Ferienzeit *(f)*, Urlaubszeit *(f)*; vacation post ⟨*AE*⟩: Ferienbeschäftigung *(f)*; vacation replacement: Urlaubsvertretung *(f)*; vacation schedule: Urlaubsplan *(m)*; vacation work: Ferienarbeit *(f)*.

vaccination certificate — Impfschein *(m)*.

validation period — Gültigkeitsdauer *(f)*.

validity — Gültigkeit *(f)*.

versatility training — Vielseitigkeitstraining *(n)*.

victimise *(v)* — schikanieren.

visual display unit *(VDU)* — Bildschirmgerät *(n)*.

vocation — Beruf *(m)*, Berufung *(f)*.

vocational *(adj)* — beruflich; vocational advancement: Berufsförderung *(f)*; vocational advice department: Berufsberatungsstelle *(f)*; vocational choice: Berufswahl *(f)*; vocational counseling/guidance: Berufsberatung *(f)*; vocational guidance center: Berufsberatungsstelle *(f)*; vocational training: Berufsausbildung *(f)*, Fachausbildung *(f)*; Vocational Training Act: Berufsbildungsgesetz *(n)*.

void *(adj)* — nichtig.

voluntary *(adj)* — freiwillig.

volunteer — Volontär *(m)*.

vote *(v)* — abstimmen.

vote — Stimme *(f)*, Abstimmung *(f)*; initial vote: Urabstimmung *(f)*.

voting paper ⟨*AE*⟩ — Stimmzettel *(m)*.

voting right — Stimmrecht *(n)*.

W

wage — ⟨*Arbeits-*⟩ Lohn *(m)*; wage account: Lohnkonto *(n)* wage adjustment: Lohnangleichung *(f)*, Lohnausgleich *(m)*; wage administration: Lohnverwaltung *(f)*; wage agreement: Lohntarifvertrag *(m)*; wage assignment: Lohnabtretung *(f)*; wage attachment: Lohnpfändung *(f)*; wage claim/demand: Lohnforderung *(f)*; wage classification: Lohneingruppierung *(f)*; wage cost accounting: Lohnrechnung *(f)*; wage costs *(Pl)*: Lohnaufwendungen *(f, Pl)*, Lohnkosten *(Pl)*; wage cut: Lohnkürzung *(f)*; wage determination: Lohnfestsetzung *(f)*; wage differential: Lohngefälle *(n)*, Abstand der Lohngruppen untereinander; wage dispute: Lohnstreitigkeit *(f)*; wage earner: Lohnempfänger(in) *(m* ⟨*f*⟩*)*; wage equalisation fund: Lohnausgleichskasse *(f)*; wage fluctuation: Lohnbewegung *(f)*; wage grade/group: Lohnstufe *(f)*,

Lohngruppe *(f)*; wage incentive: Lohnanreiz *(m)*; wage income: Lohneinkommen *(n)*; wage increase/rise/raise ⟨AE⟩: Lohnerhöhung *(f)*; wage increment: Lohnzuwachs *(m)*; wage index: Lohnindex *(m)*; wage level: Lohnniveau *(n)*; wage per hour: Stundenlohn *(m)*; wage policy: Lohnpolitik *(f)*; wage rate: Lohnrate *(f)*, Lohnsatz *(m)*; wage rate bracket: Tarifklasse *(f)* wage rate structure: Tarifstruktur *(f)*; wage scale: Lohnskala *(f)*, Rahmentarif *(m)*; wage schedule: Lohntabelle *(f)*, Tarifordnung *(f)*; wage setting: Lohnfestsetzung *(f)*; wage slip: Lohnzettel *(m)*, Lohnstreifen *(m)*; wage stop/freeze: Lohnstop *(m)*, Einfrieren *(n)* der Löhne; wage structure: Lohngefüge *(n)*, Lohnstruktur *(f)*; wage structure agreement: Lohnrahmentarifvertrag *(m)*; wage supplement: Lohnzulage *(f)*; wage total: Lohnsumme *(f)*; wage(s) advance: Lohnvorschuß *(m)*; wage(s) collective bargaining: Lohnverhandlungen *(f, Pl)*; wage(s) curve: Lohnkurve *(f)*; wage(s) cut: Lohnkürzung; wage(s) statement: Lohnabrechnung *(f)*; wage(s) tax: Lohnsteuer *(f)*; wage(s) tax card/sheet: Lohnsteuerkarte *(f)*; wage(s) tax refund: Lohnsteuerrückerstattung *(f)*; wage-control(ing) committee: Lohnkommission *(f)*; wage-dependent *(adj)*: lohnabhängig; wages council/board/committee: Tarifausschuß *(m)*, Lohnausschuß *(m)*; wages lost: Lohnausfall *(m)*; wageworker ⟨AE⟩: Lohnarbeiter(in) *(m ⟨f⟩)*, Lohnempfänger(in) *(m ⟨f⟩)*.

waiting period — Wartezeit *(f)*.

walk out *(v)* — Arbeit niederlegen, streiken.

walking delegate ⟨AE⟩ — Gewerkschaftsfunktionär(in) *(m ⟨f⟩)*.

walkout ⟨AE⟩ — Arbeitsniederlegung *(f)*.

want ads ⟨AE⟩ — Stellengesuche *(n, Pl)* ⟨Zeitungsüberschrift⟩.

war disablement — Kriegsbeschädigung *(f)*.

war pension — Kiegsbeschädigtenrente *(f)*.

war resister — Kriegsdienstverweigerer *(m)*.

warehouse keeper — Lagerverwalter(in) *(m ⟨f⟩)*.

warehouse laborer ⟨AE⟩ — Lagerarbeiter(in) *(m ⟨f⟩)*.

warning — Verwarnung *(f)*; warning strike: Warnstreik *(m)*.

warranty — Bürgschaft *(f)*, Garantie *(f)*.

washout ⟨colloq.⟩ — Versager *(m)*.

wave of strikes — Streikwelle *(f)*.

way of living — Lebensart *(f)*, Lebenswandel *(m)*.

weekday — Wochentag *(m)*.

weekly pay — Wochenlohn *(m)*.

welfare — Wohlfahrt *(f)*, Fürsorge *(f)*; welfare benefits *(Pl)*: Fürsorgeleistungen *(f, Pl)*; welfare recipient: Fürsorgeempfänger(in) *(m ⟨f⟩)*; welfare services *(Pl)*: Sozialeinrichtung *(f)*.

well-to-do *(adj)* — kaufkräftig.

white collar worker ⟨colloq.⟩ — Angestellte(r) *(f ⟨m⟩)*.

white collar union — Angestelltengewerkschaft *(f)*.

wholesale merchant — Großhandelskaufmann *(m)*.

wholesaler — Großhandelskaufmann *(m)*.

widow's benefit ⟨BE⟩ — Hinterbliebenenbezüge *(m, Pl)*.

willing *(adj)* **to work** — arbeitswillig.

withdrawal of termination — Kündigungsrücknahme *(f)*.

withhold *(v)* — abhalten, zurückhalten; withholding exemption: Freibetrag *(m)*

⟨*Lohnsteuer*⟩; withholding statement ⟨*AE*⟩: Lohnsteuerkarte *(f)*; withholding tax: Lohn-/Einkommensteuer *(f)*.

women's housework day — Hausarbeitstag *(m)*.

work — Arbeit *(f)*, Dienst *(m)*, Tätigkeit *(f)*, Werk *(n)*; be *(v)* at work: arbeiten; work *(v)* short time: kurzarbeiten; work accident: Betriebsunfall *(m)*; work according to the book ⟨*AE*⟩: planmäßiges Langsamarbeiten *(n)*; work area: Arbeitsbereich *(m)*; work at night: Nachtarbeit *(f)*; work(ing) clothes *(Pl)*: Arbeitskleidung *(f)*; work content: Arbeitsinhalt *(m)*; work cycle: Taktzeit *(f)*; work done by minors: Jugendarbeit *(f)*; work done by nonstrikers: Streikarbeit *(f)*; work dress: Arbeitskleidung *(f)*; work experience: Berufserfahrung *(f)*; work flow/routine: Arbeitsablauf *(m)*; work(ing) organisation: Arbeitsorganisation *(f)*; work order: Arbeitsauftrag *(m)*; work period: Arbeitsschicht *(f)*; work permit: Arbeitserlaubnis *(f)*; work(ing) place: Arbeitsplatz *(m)*, Arbeitsort *(m)*; work regulations *(Pl)*: Arbeitsordnung *(f)*, Betriebsordnung; work report: Arbeitsbericht *(m)*; work satisfaction: Arbeitszufriedenheit *(f)*; work sequence: Arbeitsfolge *(f)*; work shift: Arbeitsschicht *(f)*; work speed: Arbeitstempo *(n)*; work standards *(Pl)*: Arbeits(zeit)vorgaben *(f, Pl)*; work stoppage: Arbeitsniederlegung *(f)*; work to rule ⟨*BE*⟩: planmäßiges Langsamarbeiten *(n)*, Dienst *(m)* nach Vorschrift; work urge: Arbeitseifer *(m)*.

workday — Werktag *(m)*.

worker — Arbeiter(in) *(m* ⟨*f*⟩*)*; worker participation: Arbeitnehmer-Mitbeteiligung; workers' council: Betriebsrat *(m)*; workers' director: Arbeitsdirektor *(m)*; workers' protection law: Arbeitsschutzgesetz *(n)*.

workforce — Belegschaft *(f)*.

working — Tätigkeit *(f)*, Arbeiten *(n)*, Schaffen *(n)*; working capacity: Arbeitskraft *(f)*; working class: Arbeiterklasse *(f)*; working class family: Arbeiterfamilie *(f)*; working conditions *(Pl)*: Arbeitsbedingungen *(f, Pl)* ⟨*äußere*⟩; working cycle: Arbeitstakt *(m)* ⟨*Maschine*⟩; working day: Arbeitstag *(m)*; working hour: Arbeitsstunde *(f)*; working lunch: Arbeitsessen *(n)*; working morale: Arbeitsmoral *(f)*; working papers *(Pl)*: Arbeitspapiere *(n, Pl)*; working party ⟨*BE*⟩: Arbeitsgruppe *(f)*; working process: Arbeitsverfahren *(n)*, Arbeitsablauf *(m)*; working schedule/scheme: Arbeitsplan *(m)*; working system: Arbeitsmethode *(f)*; working time reduction: Arbeitszeitverkürzung *(f)*; Working Time Regulation: Arbeitszeitordnung *(f)*.

workload — Arbeitsbelastung *(f)*, Arbeitsumfang *(m)*.

workman — Arbeiter *(m)*, Arbeitskraft *(f)*.

workmanship — Arbeitsausführung *(f)*.

workmate — Arbeitskollege *(m)*, Arbeitskollegin *(f)*.

workmen's compensation insurance — Berufsgenossenschaft *(f)*.

Workmen's Compensation Law ⟨*AE*⟩ — Arbeiter-Unfallversicherungs-Gesetz(n).

workplace layout — Arbeitsplatzgestaltung *(f)*.

Workplace Regulations — Arbeitsstätten-Verordnung *(f)*.

works — Betriebs-, Werks-; works agreement: Betriebsvereinbarung *(f)*; works alteration: Betriebsänderung *(f)*; works assembly/meeting: Betriebsversammlung *(f)*; works committee: Betriebsausschuß *(m)* ⟨*Betriebsrat* ⟩; works constitution: Betriebsverfassung *(f)*; Works Constitution Act: Betriebsverfassungsgesetz *(n)*; works council:

Betriebsrat *(m)*; works manager ⟨*BE*⟩: Betriebsleiter *(m)*; works outing: Betriebsausflug *(m)*; works sickness fund: Betriebskrankenkasse *(f)*.

workshop — Werkstatt *(f)*.
workshy *(adj)* — arbeitsscheu.

Y

yard ⟨*AE*⟩ ⟨*colloq.*⟩ — Arbeitsplatz *(m)*.
year-end premium — Jahresabschlußvergütung *(f)*.
years of service — Betriebszugehörigkeit *(f)*, Dienstalter *(n)*.

Young Persons Protection of Employment Act — Jugendarbeitsschutzgesetz *(n)*.

Notizen

Notizen

Notizen

Notizen

Notizen